The Burden of Being a Boy

The Burden of Being a Boy

Bolstering Educational Achievement and Emotional Well-Being in Young Males

Nicholas D. Young, Christine N. Michael, and Elizabeth Jean

ROWMAN & LITTLEFIELD
Lanham • Boulder • New York • London

Published by Rowman & Littlefield
An imprint of The Rowman & Littlefield Publishing Group, Inc.
4501 Forbes Boulevard, Suite 200, Lanham, Maryland 20706
www.rowman.com

6 Tinworth Street, London SE11 5AL

Copyright © 2019 by Nicholas D. Young, Christine N. Michael, Elizabeth Jean

British Library Cataloguing in Publication Information Available

Library of Congress Cataloging-in-Publication Data

ISBN: 978-1-4758-5139-7 (cloth : alk. paper)
ISBN: 978-1-4758-5140-3 (pbk. : alk. paper)
ISBN: 978-1-4758-5141-0 (electronic)

♾ ™ The paper used in this publication meets the minimum requirements of American National Standard for Information Sciences Permanence of Paper for Printed Library Materials, ANSI/NISO Z39.48-1992.

Table of Contents

Preface

The Burden of Being a Boy: Bolstering Educational Achievement and Emotional Well-Being in Young Males is written for everyone who has a stake in the health and well-being of contemporary American boys and adolescents—parents, educators, counselors, educational administrators, student services personnel, higher education faculty, and students studying education and psychology. Mainly though, this is a book for those who are committed to seeing all boys grow and thrive while avoiding what has been termed as toxic male culture in this, and other, countries. While this book largely focuses on understanding the roles that schooling and upbringing play on boys' development, it explores this complex topic with a clear belief that there are myriad factors that influence each boy's developmental trajectory and that there are many ways to promote healthy, prosocial development among all young men.

The word "burden" may seem overly dramatic in the description of the state of contemporary boyhood, but there is no denying that boys are in trouble. This is evidenced in their lower achievement in schools, higher rates of physical and gun violence, increasing mental health issues, and lesser levels of enrollment in and persistence to graduation in institutions of higher education when compared to females. Yet, boys and boy culture often are misunderstood; they have strong emotions, connections, friendships, and dreams, but often express them in a language or act upon them in ways that appear inscrutable to their earliest teacher, their parents, and societal institutions in general. Deciphering the boy code and responding to boys' needs is critical if we are to help young men flourish.

Much has been written about the recent failures of males in American society; while this book presents a portrait and statistics and trends that reflect this failure, the authors are most interested in delving into the inner worlds of boys in order to better understand their emotional lives, the things that matter most to them, their ways of making meaning, and their identity needs. Given that they have unique educational and emotional needs that often go unaddressed, boys must be the recipients of new approaches to academic engagement, post-secondary achievement, counseling, health, and well-being strategies that have goodness of fit.

Slocumb's 2007 book entitled *The Boys in Crisis* asks readers to "hear our cry" that comes from the depths of pain, poverty, underachievement, and misunderstanding. As Slocumb (2007) points out, statistics on boys and young men prove that their social and emotional and mental health needs have been ignored. If this trend continues, more and more young males will be on track for shorter lifespans, less personal and professional success, and greater risk for mental health problems and incarceration. Further, they cannot fulfill their potential to raise up the next generation of boys into promise and prosocial behavior.

Despite this allegedly being a "man's world," the truth is that for so many American boys, the future holds a dreary scenario. Boys and young males are far more likely than their female counterparts to be involved in the juvenile justice system, be incarcerated, belong to a gang, die from suicide, be killed unintentionally or by homicidal means, be raised with an emotionally or physically absent father, or drop out of school. They are less likely to graduate from college or attend graduate school.

Jolliff and Horne (1999) add to this list, citing the fact that boys are assigned to special education or other special classes in school, referred for more disciplinary actions, receive lower grades throughout their schooling, and are held back in grade more often than girls.

The motivation for writing this book comes from several concerns:

- Our recognition that boys are underachieving in schools at rates that surpass those of their female counterparts;
- Our concern that while access to post-secondary education has increased, graduation rates for males, especially from underserved populations, have not;
- Our belief that boys are disproportionately represented in school disciplinary proceedings and special education designations and that boys of color are even further misrepresented as compared to the general population;
- Our awareness that schools, especially in the elementary grades, are less likely to be populated by male teachers, mentors, and role models who teach in ways that best support boys' learning preferences;
- Our knowledge that boys are bright, fiercely loyal, emotional beings who deserve a deeper understanding of their unique ways of expressing those emotions, bonds, and connections to others; and

- Our understanding that, in the face of mounting mental and emotional health issues among young males, intervention strategies and counseling approaches that are tailored to the needs and preferences of boys and men must be developed and implemented in order to promote prosocial development

This book seeks to understand the variables complicating male development in contemporary society and stresses strategies and stances that may help ease the developmental passages. It begins with an overview of salient theories of male development in Western culture, noting influences on the internalization of the "boy code" and other aspects of maleness. The authors discussed the various ways in which boys are taught from early on to tamp down many emotions and basic needs in order to meet the social standards of what it is to be male. In the process of identity formation, many boys are forced to give up or submerge aspects of self in order to fit in.

Special attention will be paid to improving boys' educational engagement and attainment. Consideration will also be given to social, cultural, and sexual diversity as well as considering the frightening increases in male violence—against others and self. Such incidences as school shootings, bullying (both face-to-face and in cyberspace), self-injury, and suicide attend the formative years of boys at far higher rates than girls. Chapters reflect current thinking on the best ways to break the cycle of early violence in order to prevent later incidents of domestic violence and acts of aggression against others.

The reader will be left with an expanded understanding of the educational and emotional needs of boys and adolescents, as well as of the educational programs and practices that can be employed to successfully engage them in their schooling. Promising practices for improving mental and emotional health, as well as strategies for effective counseling and mentoring will also be considered. Parenting that encourages young males to embrace their emotional lives, friendships, and unique identities are explored as well.

The topics noted above are the major foci of the chapters of this book. In writing this book, the authors attempt to reach an integration of theory, scholarly research, and empirically based best practices that have utility for those working with boys and young men. Using developmental psychology, cultural studies, and educational theory and practice to understand the current definitions and implications of masculinity in American society, the authors offer proactive, prosocial solutions to the limiting or destructive aspects of "male culture." This book should support the work of all who care about the future of young males and hope to maximize their potential to be "whole" men.

The Burden of Being a Boy: Bolstering Educational Achievement and Emotional Well-Being in Young Males is written by an experienced team of educators who have interacted with boys in a variety of roles during their careers. Having experienced these relationships in pre-K–12 settings, higher education, counseling, coaching, and parenting, they bring a multifaceted lens to their writing. A truncated review of appropriate scholarly literature and research studies, as well as suggestions for how to translate these into strategies to guide professional practice, are included in each of the book's chapters.

We hope that those who currently work with, educate, counsel, or are raising boys will find the book useful and reassuring in its celebration of their strengths and the joy that can be derived from interactions with young men of all economic backgrounds, races, ethnicities, and sexual orientations.

Acknowledgment

It is with sincere appreciation and respect that we offer our public thank you to Sue Clark for her superb editing of this manuscript. She is a talented member of our team of authors who has seen many of our book projects successfully to this finish line. Particular to the subject of this book, it is noteworthy that Sue has successfully raised a grown family that includes sons and that she is currently a grandmother to, among others, active young boys who are still in the process of trying to survive childhood. May she someday be rewarded for all the efforts she has expended in helping the males in her life become the kind of men that she knows they are all capable of being. And may all others know that we value her words of wisdom and innumerable contributions to this book. We could not imagine having had had a better partner or friend to assist us with completing this project. You are the best, Sue.

Chapter One

Growing Up Guy

Theories of Male Development

Throughout history, there have been many theories of male development; however, their commonalities stem from the fact that the term "human development" was essentially synonymous with "middle class, white, male development." Prominent developmental theorists such as Erikson (1980), Vaillant (1998), and Levinson (1978) articulate stage theories of men's passages through the life cycle that shared similar characteristics. Stage theories, by their very nature, were built on assumptions of universality, sequentiality, teleology, and adaptation (Cherry, 2019).

Universality meant that all humans underwent the same stages and developmental tasks throughout their lives. Sequentiality meant that the stages unfolded in the same order, creating a set of building blocks of life that were predictable. In teleology, theorists believed that individuals entered and exited these stages at roughly the same chronological ages in their lives (Oxford Dictionaries, 2019). Each stage contained developmental tasks or homework that the man needed to accomplish and, through adaptation, he moved through these stages successfully only if the homework assignments were resolved favorably (Erikson, 1980).

Erikson (1980) articulates a psychosocial crisis to be resolved if the individual were to move on to the next developmental stage in a healthy fashion. In infancy the crisis involved trust versus mistrust, which if resolved successfully led to hope. Essentially, if the infant could trust a consistent caregiver, he would be able to view the world around him as secure and orderly and could feel free to express emotions, explore the environment, and rely on adults to meet his needs.

1

In early childhood the struggle was with autonomy versus shame and doubt (Erikson, 1980). In a safe and predictable universe, the child was able to begin to explore on his own, exerting will and experiencing the beginnings of agency and competence. Play age brought initiative versus guilt in which the child could develop a sense of purpose and a comfort in testing limits and separating a sense of self from that of the caregivers. School age was comprised of developing a sense of industry over feelings of inferiority, for if the child could master learning tasks, he internalized feelings of being a competent being who could achieve his goals (Erikson, 1980).

Adolescence tasked the young man with forming an identity that had fidelity, or consonance with his unique personality, talents, and interests. In the absence of such a consolidated identity he was doomed to flounder in society. Young adulthood brought with it the quest for intimacy through forming a love relationship, marrying, and starting a family (Erikson, 1980).

Erikson's (1980) stages of development have important implications for boys and adolescent males. Infant boys who do not have their needs met are unable to form trusting relationships with others (Erikson, 1980). In the second stage, the primary work is achieving autonomy, but this can be hampered in two ways. Either the young boy is overprotected and doesn't get opportunities to explore his environment, take on challenges, or even fail; or the boy may be pushed into autonomous acts before he is ready and therefore experience too much failure or pain or even injury (physical or psychological). This can lead to shame and doubt (Horne and Kiselica, 1999).

In the industry stage, boys need to find a sense of competence, and they do this through competition with themselves and others, sometimes even their parents (Erikson, 1980). This can be successfully resolved through support and appropriate challenge or thwarted if parents are too competitive or if they are helicopter parents who never let their sons make their own decisions. In adolescence, the task is moving toward a consolidated identity and this includes separation from dependency on parents and trying out new roles and identities (Erikson, 1980). Boys can either be permitted these activities, while still feeling parents' love and support, or they can be stymied if they are held in old patterns of behavior/belief or if parents feel threatened by their growing independence (Horne and Kiselica, 1999).

Levinson (1978), in his historic work, *The Seasons of a Man's Life*, looks at the tasks of male adulthood as beginning with the formation of "the dream"—a vision of one's self in the world that fills the dreamer with energy and vitality. This "dream" animates the man's studies and work as a young person; yet, it needs to be aided by a mentor, whose chief role is to help the young man make manifest his "dream" (Levinson, 1978). The mentor generally is eight to fifteen years senior to the young man and takes him under his wing to teach, advise, model, sponsor, and support him as he develops; his task includes helping him transition both to adulthood and into the world of work (Levinson, 1978). Part father figure, part peer, this older mentor eases the young man's transition away from family of origin and into self-reliance.

Levinson's (1978) young men also benefit from another kind of guidance as they navigate early adulthood—that from the "Special Woman." Like the mentor, the "Special Woman" embraces the young man's "dream," shares in it, offers her blessing, and creates what Levinson (1978) calls "a boundary space within which his aspirations can be imagined, and his hopes nurtured" (p. 109). As a transitional figure, the "Special Woman" helps the young man "outgrow the little boy in himself and to become a more autonomous adult" (p. 109).

Models that may have operated logically in Erikson (1980), Vaillant (1998), and Levinson's (1978) times seem to have less validity in contemporary times, as these mentors, role models, and helpmates are less plentiful, or are absent completely, leaving boys and young men less supported in their development than they might have been in earlier societies (Garringer, 2004). The same is true for the "Special Woman," as she may, in modern times, be occupied with her own "dream" and be less able to fully devote herself to supporting the young man's transition. Absent formal mentoring, apprenticeships, and the modeling and discipline instilled during military service, present-day young men are frequently left to approximate their own transitions to adulthood.

Vaillant (1998) has presided over one of the most consistent longitudinal studies of development in history. Called the Grant Study and conducted through Harvard University, he and other researchers followed 268 men who entered college during the late 1930s through their lifespans, which involved wartime experiences, careers, marriages and divorces, child rearing, and later life (Vaillant, 1998). His study illustrates what made men successful and happy in their lives and included John F. Kennedy as a participant (Vaillant, 1998).

The study presents a rich treasure trove of findings, among them that Erikson's (1980) model fit the men studied relatively well; however, Vaillant (1998) found it necessary to add a new stage after Intimacy versus Isolation, that he dubbed Career Consolidation. He likened his thirty-year-old subjects in this stage to elementary school children working through the earlier Industry versus Inferiority crisis. They struggle to reconcile conforming to others' expectations of them and rarely stop to reflect on the worth of what they were doing. Their energies at this period are diverted away from their families and spouses. It was, Vaillant (1998) muses, as if they had traded in their lunchboxes for briefcases.

Vaillant's (1998) work also highlights the powerful influence of mentors in male development and the use of "adaptations" or "defense mechanisms" in their successes. Most commonly, suppression and sublimation were deployed to promote men to positions of power and success. Sadly, the men's descriptions of their intimate relationships explain much of the "father hunger" and lack of availability to their growing sons that is discussed later (Vaillant, 1998).

In their twenties and thirties, these men saw their energies primarily devoted to finding a mate and consolidating their careers; therefore, in their forties and fifties, they were able to focus on their children. Like trains passing in the night, however, they missed crucial availability during developmental periods in which their sons needed their warmth, presence, role modeling, and mentoring the most.

The aforementioned loss of availability is particularly wrenching given that Vaillant (1998) discovered that a key to greater satisfaction in later life correlated with the warmth of childhood relationships with fathers. This also correlated with lower rates of adult anxiety; however, men's childhood relationships with mothers played a far greater role in their adult well-being, in all spheres, as fathers were so frequently absent or marginal players in their childhood and adolescence (Vaillant, 1998).

SEPARATING FROM THE FEMININE

A primary task represented in so many theories, and in contemporary society, is the separation from the mother (as the representation of all things feminine). While both boys and girls need to experience incremental stages of healthy separation from parents in order to individuate or form a more independent sense of self-in-the-world, this task is experienced differently for boys and girls. Separating from parents also eases the transition from the world of home to the world of school. It is the child's way of demonstrating maturity and is a significant developmental accomplishment; however, as Chu (2014) notes:

> Beyond demonstrating maturity, however, a boy's ability (or inability) to separate easily from his mother in particular—and to deny his need for the kind of nurturance and care that the mother-child relationship represents—is believed to have further implications for his ability to establish and develop a "healthy" masculine identity. (p. 75)

Chu (2014) relates that psychoanalytic theory stresses that during early childhood, boys must separate from mother's feminine influence in order to identify with the father and acquire his masculine qualities. To fail to do this is to become a mama's boy, or not a real man, and failure relegates the boy to a low position in the social hierarchy of boys.

A critical hitch in modern male development, however, is that so many boys grow up without their fathers in their lives, with men who are geographically and/or emotionally absent. As boys enter the educational system, with its dearth of male teachers and mentors in most elementary schools, they have few places to look for models of how to become masculine. This gives boys' peers and peer groups tremendous power in socializing male children to become masculine. As Chu (2014) writes:

> In their desire to identify with their peers (e.g., be one of the boys) and relate to their peers (e.g., be with the boys), boys learn both to emphasize qualities and display behaviors that liken them to other boys and to downplay or conceal those that set them apart. In cultures and societies where masculinity is defined in contrast to, or as the opposite of, femininity, boys also learn to show that they are boys (and not girls) by distancing and differentiating themselves from girls, women, and anything associated with femininity. (p. 63)

Robertson and Shepard (2008) discuss Mahler's work on the separation-individuation process that is the foundation of most textbooks on human development. In this model, individuals move from the fusion of primary caregiver in infancy, to "rapprochement," the period of tentative exploration, and then move back and forth from the caregiver until they feel secure enough to take the first steps toward individuation—possibly because the bond with the caregiver has now been internalized (Mahler, Pine, and Bergman, 2000). This separation process may begin prematurely for many boys because their caregivers feel they must "toughen them up" or want to avoid their acting "like a girl" (Mahler, Pine, and Bergman, 2000).

Some authors, such as Pollack (1995) see this process as causing psychic wounds among boys because their needs for closeness and dependency are very real but the boys receive the message that they should not express them. This is where Bergman (1995) sees males turning away from connection, from the notion of self-in-relation. As boys become more competent in autonomy, they become less competent relationally (Bergman, 1995).

HAVIGHURST: DEVELOPMENTAL TASKS OF ADOLESCENCE

There are some predictable developmental tasks that all adolescent boys must go through, although each may experience them in unique ways and many of these are experienced simultaneously. The most difficult realization, as Gurian (1999) points out, is that adolescence can begin as early as nine and last well into the early twenties, so parents and teachers must recognize and support individual differences in how this stage is experienced.

The first changes that adolescent boys go through are physical, with the most profound since their birth. Height, weight, body changes, and the accentuation of physical traits that make them male all occur at a rapid pace. This is a time in which boys' transition to looking far more like physically and sexually mature males than like boys. Incorporating a sense of one's sexuality and values around that occupies developmental energies. Males' brain structure and biochemistry differ from girls' and these differences need to be understood. This is also a time of deep discovery for many who are gender nonconforming or questioning their sexual orientation.

Like physical growth, Havighurst (1963) postulates that adolescence would be a time of increased cognitive abilities, especially in the area of abstract thinking, although recent studies such as Jensen and Nutt (2015) and Walsh (2014) suggest that abstract thought and the ability to recognize the consequences of actions may not be developed until much later. Many adults view secondary school as preparation for career, post-secondary education, and taking on of adult roles and responsibilities. Since the curriculum of secondary school is based upon these premises, many adolescent boys will be challenged (and often frustrated) by the requirements of higher levels of formal thought. With this comes the expectation for expanded verbal skills, as well, with boys still lagging behind girls in expressive language skills, particularly in areas of emotional expression (Cox, 2006).

Identity formation and the recognition of a self that is separating from parents and community of origin are tasks for adolescent boys to ponder. Questions such as "Who am I?" and "What do I want my adult self to be?" have primacy. These lead to questions of vocation, as men are expected to enter the workforce and be providers (Parker and Stepler, 2017). While it is important to establish degrees of emotional and psychological independence from one's family of origin during adolescence, many earlier models of male development saw individuation as critical to masculinity; therefore, institutions such as apprenticing, entering the military, or missions or travel served to disrupt ties to home and thrust the young man into the larger universe.

Historically, and even today, adolescent boys have been pushed to individuate earlier and more fully than girls; yet, psychologists know that all teens waver between wanting to be more independent and desiring to keep ties to family and familiar, comfortable relationships and routines. Forming stable, positive peer relationships is a critical task for adolescent males, as this is a stage in which friends take on perhaps the most powerful developmental roles of any individuals (Havighurst, 1963).

Without friends and a positive peer group around him, a young male is at greater risk for maladjustment in other social and psychological venues (Havighurst, 1963). During adolescence, young males must also form an initial, integrated set of values and morals that guide behavior. They are forced to weigh parental, community, and cultural values against those of their peers and of larger society (Havighurst, 1963). If they can achieve this reconciliation, they form a coherent personal ideology that provides a moral compass.

In adolescence, most young people engage in one or more behaviors that pose potential physical, social, or educational risk. This is even more a part of the boy code than that of the developmental process of female adolescence

(Havighurst, 1963). Risk-taking generally is at a peak during early and middle adolescence and wanes as adolescence ends because young or emerging adults gradually settle into a set of behavioral self-controls that prompt behavior that is more like that of adults (Havighurst, 1963).

"BOY CODE" IN AMERICA

Pollack's 1998 classic book on listening to boys' voices presents a painful overview of the effects of trying to live up to boy code in America. Drawn from years of clinical practice and Harvard-based qualitative research, Pollack (1998) argues for a close examination of the cultural "straight jacket" that strangles boys' inner proclivities toward connection and forces them to live behind a mask. This code is both strong and subtle and is so powerful yet invisible that boys may not even be aware that they are living in accordance with it (Pollack, 1998).

There are four main "injunctions" in boy code that are learned and reinforced in such institutions as schools, churches, camps, sports venues, and playgrounds (Pollack, 1998). Stereotyped male "ideals" are drilled into boys' psyches from an early age. These ideals teach boys what "real men" are supposed to be like.

- The first ideal is called the "sturdy oak" and is an image of masculinity in which stoicism and independence are prized. In order to hide their natural emotions, boys wear a mask that projects only confidence and autonomy. Psychically, this can be exhausting.
- The second stereotype is called "give 'em hell" and derives from the myth that boys are biologically predisposed to high energy and risky behaviors; thus, society appears to tolerate, perhaps even encourage, the acting out of such behaviors, believing them to be the normal stuff of masculinity.
- "The big wheel" connotes the pressures for boys to achieve status, dominance, and power while avoiding losing face under all circumstances. Boys are severely censured if they display feminine qualities such as warmth, empathy, or emotion.
- The fourth dictate is "no sissy stuff." Essentially, boys are told that masculinity is anything not feminine. The fear of appearing feminine or homosexual is so strong that boys repress parts of themselves in order to measure up.

Although not part of Pollack's (1998) code, another mandate that might be added to this list is "boys are tough, not smart." Liu, Shepard, and Nicpon (2008) chart the problems of boys who fall into the gifted and talented category. While the authors stress that there are more difficulties that face this distinct population of males, they also remark that as a society, we socialize boys to believe that it is not "cool" or masculine to be too smart or to appear to be trying too hard academically. Those attitudes are relegated to girl behavior.

Being a smart boy, Fleming and Englar-Carlson (2008) opine, is even more problematic for certain subgroups of males. The authors discuss this problem as it relates to African American boys and young males, noting that they face a conflict between conforming to group standards between two disparate groups. In African American peer groups, striving for academic achievement is rarely rewarded or accepted by boys as being synonymous with masculinity, bright boys who wish to excel have to deal with the emotional stress of being scorned by their peers or not living up to their potential (Fleming and Englar-Carlson, 2008). Further, in many parts of the country, they may be a distinct minority presence in advanced classes or gifted and talented programs.

Pollack (1998; 2001) charts the beginning of socialization to the boy code in early childhood, when they are prematurely and abruptly torn from their natural connections to their mothers. As mothers remain the primary caregivers in most societies, boys are forced into wrenching themselves from their mothers in order to establish their initial "gender identity" (Pollack, 1998). While it is deemed appropriate for girls to remain closely bonded to their mothers, boys are essentially threatened with separating and developing a clear, masculine identity.

Such a rupture, based on society's prizing of male independence, may be difficult enough; considering the psychological and physical absence of so many fathers, the task of fully integrating a healthy male identity becomes further confounded (Pollack, 1998). Their whole socialization process at this young age appears to be heavily influenced by the societal dictate that they become different from women and anything associated with being female.

Boys gradually become more and more distanced from their authentic selves as they are taught to harden themselves and deaden themselves to emotional pain. Additionally, Pollack (1998) points out, society is more tolerant of girls' displaying an interest in "male" activities than it is of boys who prefer "female" activities. Homophobia runs rampant in society and plays a powerful role in tamping down young boys' natural inclination toward connection and nurturing (Pollack, 1998; 2001). Boys' inherent longing for connectedness is countered by powerful societal shaming, with "shame" being described as the feeling state that accompanies an emotional disconnect (Pollack, 1998). While girls may be sensitive to shame, Pollack (1998) argues, boys are conditioned to fear it:

> Boys are shame-phobic: they are exquisitely yet unconsciously attuned to any signal of "loss of face" and will do just about whatever it takes to avoid shame. Rather than expose themselves to this kind of potent embarrassment, boys, in

the face of suffering, engage in a variety of behaviors that range from avoidance of dependency to impulsive action, from bravado and rage-filled outbursts to intense violence. (p. 33)

There is a second separation that occurs in adolescence and early adulthood. At this point, boys are defined by the degrees of separation from their family; however, contemporary society presents a mixed message to them in asking them to take on roles of the "new male" while living up to the old male codes:

It is not impossible to be both manly and empathic, cool and open, strong and vulnerable, but it is certainly a difficult and complex task. Most boys have a very difficult time trying to sort out these conflicting messages and determining what masculine model to pattern themselves after. (Pollack, 1998, p. 146)

Boys are further misunderstood and hampered in their development due to cultural stereotypes about them. Pollack (1998; 2001) contends that there are three powerful myths that adversely affect how society views and reacts to contemporary boys. The first myth is that "boys will be boys" that "nature," biology, and specifically testosterone are more influential agents affecting boys' behavior than anything that individuals or institutions can do to shape them. In effect, believing this myth results in people's false assumptions that "they have less power to affect a boy's personality, behavior, or emotional development than in fact they do" (Pollack, 2001, p. 53).

While Pollack (2001) does not dispute the role that testosterone can play, behavior can be cultivated and channeled into positive, and even connected, ways of being in the world. Boys, he says, are deeply in need of connection:

Parents and others who love and look after boys, are empowered in their efforts by their boys' own deep yearning for connection. This is what I call "the potency of connection." The power of love can dispel the myth that, in adolescence, boys' nature and nurture are at odds, or, indeed have distinct separate influences on a boy and his life. The way we interact with boys, and the connections we make with them, can have a permanent effect on a boy's biology, his brain and his social behavior. Scientists have found that early emotional interaction can actually alter a boy's brain-based biological processes. (p. 56)

A second myth that he debunks is that it is imperative that boys be "macho" in order to make it in society. This myth prevents parents and significant others from nurturing unique temperament, personality, and proclivities of boys out of fear that they will not turn out to be "manly" enough. Pollack (1998) argues that diversity in masculinity and its expression is as prevalent as cultural diversity, and that culture, history, and social factors play roles in determining what is considered "healthy manhood" in any given context.

The final, perhaps saddest, myth is that "boys are toxic." Rittenmeyer (2002) describes it as follows:

> Put aside for the moment the double standard of how teenage girls joke about the "bulge" in a football player's pants but are unlikely to be branded as sexual harassers and ask why we have confused boys' childish exploratory play with adult predatory behavior. No doubt some components of boys' and girls' play go beyond the bounds of acceptability and are deserving of redirection or even reprimand. Yet, when it is a boy involved, we seem to forget his need to play, experiment, and fail in order to grow. Instead we respond as though he is a full-fledged aggressor. (p. 43)

Rittenmeyer's 2002 doctoral dissertation on the "heroic journey" of adolescent boys is perhaps one of the most telling research studies about the inner lives of teenage males. Using phenomenological interviews, lengthy discussions were conducted with boys about their life experiences in high school. The findings refute the notion that boys are stoic creatures who "thrive on solitude" (Rittenmeyer, 2002, p. 105). Quite to the contrary, the boys interviewed told emotional stories, even if they struggled at times to find the language to express their experiences. Analyzing their texts, Rittenmeyer (2002) found common themes that cut across their adolescent experiences. First, their stories were rich in what was described as "communion themes." This is surprising, given that communion themes are more often associated with femininity (Rittenmeyer, 2002).

Friendships and connection were powerful needs expressed by co-researchers; however, they were expressed and experienced differently from girls' friendships, as Rittenmeyer (2002) argues that,

> girls' friendships may appear significantly different than boys' friendships but in spirit they are just as intimate and meet the same needs. One of the S's in this study talked about the difference. His philosophy was that guys would always be there for you, no matter what, because they're not as possessive about their relationships as girls are. As each S in the study talked about his most significant moments his friends were interwoven throughout the narrative. (p. 115)

Boys reached out to their friends in times of sadness, worry, or doubt, or their friends reached out to them if they saw them in need; however, this took place most often in more private settings, rather than in the more public dramas that girls played out. Sadly, the same close helping relationships could not be said for adults in boys' lives. As Rittenmeyer (2002) notes, "the mere absence of the supporting role of parents in the stories is concerning" (p. 116).

This research supported the findings of Pollack (1998) and Lamb (1995) in stressing boys' desire for connection with parents, especially close relationships with their fathers. Why this connection was missing was not evident from the study's findings; however, Rittenmeyer (2002) conjectures that it may be due to parents who have fallen for the myth that boys don't need connection as much as their daughters do, or that they believe that boys must be "toughened" up emotionally in order to make it in the male world, and thus begin to distance themselves from warmer relationships with boys in order not to "sissify" them.

In any case, Rittenmeyer (2002) found that "there is no doubt that the S's in this study were capable of being very hurt by adults. It was particularly upsetting to them when they felt that they were not being understood and accepted for who they were" (p. 119). These findings validate Pollack's (1998) statement that boys have "deep subliminal yearnings for connection [that may not be expressed as girls might express them, but that are truly] a hidden yearning for relationship that makes them long to be close to teachers, coaches, friends and family" (p. 18).

Rittenmeyer (2002) was somewhat surprised not to find a strong emphasis on themes of power, autonomy, mastery, independence, and achievement, as these are traditionally associated with masculinity. Boys were mostly balanced between agentic and communion needs, with a slight tip toward communion. It appears that close ties were more important than power and autonomy, in the traditional sense. Mastery of "the environment around them and understanding how they relate to that environment were the most prominent agentic themes . . . all wanted to feel more competent and spent a great deal of time trying to figure out how to get there" (Rittenmeyer, 2002, p. 112). This type of adolescent mastery could better be understood through the boys' stories than through a stereotypical definition of mastery: boys were extremely resilient in overcoming challenges, and the support network of their friends helped to provide the safety net when taking on difficult tasks.

What is striking about Rittenmeyer's (2002) study is that the boys' stories of lived experience directly contradicted many prevalent cultural stereotypes about who boys are and what they need. Clearly, communion and connection with each other and with adults are important; boys want and need to speak about their inner worlds. They simply are hampered in finding the language to do so, perhaps because "boys have been 'silenced' by a gender role stereotype that suggests silence is developmentally normal for adolescent boys" (Rittenmeyer, 2002, p. 121).

Clearly, institutions such as schools, are failing them in ways that may have profoundly negative effects on their achievement and their sense of self-worth. An additional challenge lies in boys' inherent ambivalence about masculinity as it is currently defined:

> Boys have ambivalent feelings about male adulthood—they're not all that sure that being a man is going to be such a great experience. They may not see any male role model that appeals to them and they feel is within their reach. Must

they spend their whole lives chained to a job they don't love in order to support a family? And they may suspect that the double standard will not abate in its influence as they become adults, that they will be expected to navigate through dating, marriage, work and family-making (or choosing not to do those things) while being bombarded by similarly conflicting messages about how the ideal man behaves. (Pollack, 1998, p. 146)

Not only is the new "ideal male" stereotype confusing, but where is the adolescent to look for role models and mentors to lead him down the path toward such manhood? Certainly, for most young males, there are few, if any, such polestars in their lives; thus, making this transition an even more turbulent one. One reason for this ambivalence in boys about male adulthood is the lack of genuine polestars. Sheehy (1986) summarizes the literature on those who are resilient and who have overcome the odds to go on to full, rich lives.

In a meta-analysis of studies of those victorious individuals, they were blessed with what was called "polestars," or transformative figures upon whom the triumphant could depend (Sheehy, 1986). Older than they were, the polestar served as a proxy parent or a mentor to the young person, lighting a lamp along the path to survival.

Several decades ago, one of Levinson's (1978) graduate students who assisted in the research on male development conducted her own doctoral research. A striking feature of this replication of Levinson's work—this time conducted with young women as the research informants—was the "split dream" of so many of them.

Envisioning how to reconcile their desire for career with their desire for family was far more conflictual and perplexing than it had been for Levinson's young men. In Pollack's (1998) work, it is hard not to hear the agony of the "split self" as his adolescent boys were tested on both the Sex-Role Egalitarianism Scale (King and King, 1993) and Pleck's (1995) Traditional Male Role Attitudes Scale. As Pollack (1998) notes, "when given the opportunity to bare their souls, these adolescent boys, without knowing it, revealed an inner fissure, a split in their sense of what it means to be a man" (p. 166).

When Pollack (1998) used a variation of the Thematic Apperception Test (a picture showing a black and white sketch of a man dressed for business, reviewing papers at his work site), he found that only 15 percent of the boys told stories that put the man in the "happy, contented family man" category. Most of the other boys (35%) chose "the lonely, career-oriented man," followed by the "alienated breadwinner" (24%), and the "permanently separated man" (5%) (Pollack, 1998). Such results suggest that male adulthood may not be all that it is cracked up to be.

Boys experience a "split self" that has implications for emotional pain and distress throughout their lives if left untreated. Society in general, and counseling as a profession, must rescue boys from their socialization to inauthenticity if boys are to grow into "real men" who can partner, raise children, and fulfill generative roles in the future.

FATHERS, SONS, AND MENTORS

According to Osherson (1986) and Bergman (1995) boys begin to look for a masculine model to fashion a sense of self around the age of three. It is also at this time that they seek to "be like Daddy" and to segregate by gender. Socialized to begin to move away from a relationship with the mother in order to create a sense of male self, they are faced with what Osherson (1986) describes as a "crucial dilemma":

> Boys have to give up mother for father, but who is father? Often a shadowy figure at best, difficult to understand. Boys rarely experience fathers as sources of warm, soft nurturance. . . . If father is not there to provide a confident, rich model of manhood, then the boy is left in a vulnerable position: having to distance himself from mother without a clear and understandable model of male gender upon which to base his emerging identity. (p. 6)

Men play such a marginal role in so many families, Osherson (1986) argues, boys often misidentify with, distort, or mythologize their relationships with their fathers, leading them to carry around a "wounded father" within them during their adult lives. Fathers most often are somehow categorized as "rejecting, incompetent, or absent" (Osherson, 1986, p. 6). In his 1986 study, Osherson quotes figures that place fathers in direct relationship with their children an average of thirty-seven minutes a day when the children are three months or under, and at one hour per day when they reach nine months.

Bergman (1995) echoes this note when speaking of fathers who are absent physically, geographically, or emotionally. In their absence, their sons must make something of the mysterious father figure, and usually end up either making the father out to be larger than life (hero) or smaller than life (wimp) (Bergman, 1995, p. 77). Bergman (1995) admits that there are many wonderful father-son relationships, and many things that fathers are uniquely suited to teach their young sons.

Most often the relationship works "in valuing independence and action, in learning to do things out in the world. Often it emphasizes 'success' and what the boy does—not who a boy is, rarely who a boy is with others, and almost never who a boy is mutually with others" (Bergman, 1995, p.77). Because of their own socialization, fathers are rarely skilled at and comfortable with initiating their young sons into the relational realm or interacting around emotions; thus, they do not often teach them "affective give-and-take, continuity, and working through conflict and difference to mutual empowerment" (Bergman, 1995, p. 77).

For Osherson's (1986) research informants, adulthood was colored by their relationship with their fathers. For some, this led to shame, as they felt that they were not living up to the heroic (but usually mythical) standards that their fathers set; for others, there was a drive to avoid what they saw as passivity or ineffectiveness that their fathers had displayed. Both Osherson (1986) and Bergman (1995) agree that men are hampered in their emotional development.

Osherson (1986) writes that men "do not learn to be cared for, to get nurturance and intimacy from men" (p. 10), while Bergman (1995) believes that men are unable to practice self-care. In both cases, men expect women to care for them, rather than seeing this as a necessary part of their own repertoire of skills. Osherson's (1986) "wounded father" may negatively influence his son's development in three significant ways to include,

> The son may remember the father as wounded, with the father's deep sadness, incompetence or anger dominating his image of the man. He may also remember the father as wounding, evoking the loss and needy feelings the son experienced in having been rejected by or disappointing to the father. And thirdly, the son may introject and internalize distorted and idealized images and memories of father as he struggles to synthesize his identity as a man. (p. 27)

Four salient father images confound the father-son relationship to include: (1) the angry/disappointed father; (2) the all-suffering father; (3) the saintly or heroic father; and (4) the secretly vulnerable father (Osherson, 1986). Working things out with one's father seems essential to a man's health and well-being, yet Osherson (1986) was surprised by how many men move into adulthood by seeking "to separate from significant figures by getting distance from them without working through our intense, mixed feelings" (p. 21). Putting such distance on fathers leads men to what has been described as "father hunger" (Osherson, 1986, p. 21).

Osherson (1986), citing Vaillant's (1998) famous Grant Study, reports that "in more than ninety-five percent of cases, fathers were either cited as negative examples or were mentioned as people who were not influences" (p. 54). One way that men may fill up this hunger is by searching for a mentor-father. Cited as a powerful influence in the formation of a young man's initial life structure, mentors help the young man navigate the difficult passage from early adulthood into real adulthood (Levinson, 1978). But Osherson (1986) remarksd that mentors are most frequently found in the world of work and may reinforce some of the less desirable traits of traditional manhood:

> Unsure of their own fathers some men search for older, more senior men who will help them solidify a fragile masculine identity, which is usually of the

brittle, instrumental sort that emphasizes career achievement and public dem-
onstrations of power and strength. Such identities may lead to a withering of
the man's capacity to tolerate his own more receptive, less public, or less
action-oriented sides. (p. 54)

Mentoring relationships can be fraught with difficulty, especially for those
men who came of age during the 1960s, whose free speech slogan was
"never trust anyone over thirty" (DiGioia, 2018). The intergenerational tension spawned by that war made it difficult for young men and their mentors
to go about the traditional business of mentoring. It is also through the
mentoring relationship that many men reenact conflicts with their fathers.

Levinson (1978) deliberately titles the period of midlife male adulthood as
BOOM (becoming one's own man) and notes that it's characterized by the need
to throw off one's mentor, usually in some sort of wrenching blowup that creates
a permanent chasm between the two. This is an unconscious reliving of the
separation from father. Inherent in too many male mentoring relationships are
the simultaneous expressions of cruelty on the part of the young mentees and
"cannibalism" on the part of the older mentors (Osherson, 1986).

MODELS OF OPTIMAL MALE DEVELOPMENT
IN BOYHOOD AND ADOLESCENCE

Kiselica, Englar-Carlson, Horne, and Fisher (2008) urge a positive psychology approach to think about how to help boys and adolescent males attain
optimal development. In such an approach, one would focus on "the beauty
of boys" and take the line that it is our job to foster resiliency and emotional
health and well-being by focusing on boys' assets and virtues and building
on what is right about individuals rather than trying to remedy what is wrong
(Kiselica et al., 2008).

Kiselica et al. (2008) points to attributes that are valuable in positive male
development throughout the life cycle to include male relational styles; generative fatherhood; male ways of caring; self-reliance; the worker-provider
role; males' courage, daring and risk-taking; group orientation; the humani-
tarian service of fraternal organizations; males' humor; and heroism. Each of
these, if used as a basis for supporting boys and young males, can bolster
optimal development through building on natural male assets within the
framework of psychoeducational experiences.

The authors note that even though the image of males throughout our
history is that of "rugged individualism," boys spend more time in coordinat-
ed group activity than do girls. Boys and men are drawn to groups and this is
a natural way to structure psychoeducational activities (Kiselica et al., 2008).
Affinity groups provide shared venues for activities and preventative groups
are valuable in promoting prosocial behavior and well-being. Boys use hu-

mor to attain intimacy through joking and laughing with their friends and to show their concern for those they care about. Boys also use humor as a coping or stress-relieving tool, both for themselves and for others in their orbit. Getting a friend who is down to laugh or interjecting a joke to break a tense moment in a conflict situation are ways that boys can build connections and manage potentially stressful environments.

Male relational styles—often misunderstood or maligned—are forged out of shared experiences, action-oriented activities. They form bonds and relationships through games, sports, adventures, rather than intimate dyadic discussions. They have what has been termed "action empathy," or the ability to take action by considering another's point of view (Kiselica et al., 2008). Others note "covert" intimacy that, rather than being developed in intimate, paired discussions as with girls, arises from "emotional closeness through self-disclosure that occurs within the context of shared activities" (Kiselica et al., 2008, p. 34).

If seen through the lens of feminized intimacy, it would appear that boys are less intimate; yet, Kiselica et al. (2008) begs counselors and educators and parents to understand that boys and men undergo the same powerful human emotions, just expressed in a communal, rather than a more paired, talk-oriented way.

While many boys and adolescent males have not had the benefit of generative fathering, they can be taught about generative fathering and can experience it through relationships with mentors and other caring men in their lives. Fathers provide different and incredibly valuable ways of interacting with their children and experiencing the world with them. Generative fathers not only care for their children in developmentally appropriate ways but prepare the next generation of fathers to fulfill the role (Kiselica et al., 2008). For many men, this generative role is one of the greatest joys of their life and one of their most important contributions to society.

Traditionally, the world of work has been how men have defined themselves, providing them with purpose and meaning. Through caring economically for loved ones, men demonstrate their devotion to family and country; work has been the central core of male identity (Kiselica et al., 2008). Work and its relationship to positive masculinity is also at the core of good counseling practice and education. In one sense, since the transition to the world of work is a seminal rite of passage, we need to place greater emphasis on career education and counseling for boys and adolescent males so that they can enter that world successfully with a career path that has goodness of fit.

Work and self-esteem are often inextricably linked; thus, this is an important element of good mental health. Finally, since work ethic and task orientation are strong in boys and males, this is a good way to frame any kind of therapeutic work, by using the analogies of "jobs" and "working together" to complete the task (Kiselica et al., 2008).

Service activities have long provided males with socialization and ways to bond over task completion. Involving younger males in service learning, clubs, and community organizations can improve prosocial functioning and develop an orientation toward helping others. These can also fill functions that men play in the optimal development of boys and adolescents such as providing healthy role models, initiation, mentoring, and the passing on of societal rituals and cultural norms (Horne, Jolliff, and Roth, 1996).

It is easy to see how these various functions can be met through active membership in multigenerational service groups and activities, and these are perhaps even more important for young males suffering a dearth of fathers and other positive males in their lives. Horne et al.'s (1996) research essentially postulates an alternative model of male development in that it describes the roles of important adult males at stages of the boy's life rather than looking at the developmental tasks of stages. Nurturers, who can be fathers, or when they are absent, extended family or close friends and relatives, help provide the stability, affection, and consistency that boys need to move through the first of Erikson's (1980) stages. Role models, who can be real-life people present in the boy's life, taken from larger culture, media figures, or even characters from literature can either be positive or negative influences. The boy will internalize behavioral standards and masculine codes from those he admires; boys need abundant, positive role models through all stages of their development in order to reach mature masculinity (Horne et al., 1996).

Initiators provide a counterbalance to being self-centered or egocentric (Jolliff and Horne, 1999). They bind the boy to larger group commitments through modeling and supporting teamwork, cooperation, and group loyalty. They stress a healthy inclusion of others and a balance between cooperative and competitive urges. Initiators send the boy on the path toward self-efficacy through activities that help him internalize the standards for personal accomplishment and the ability to self-assess in relation to intended goals (Jolliff and Horne, 1999). Since contemporary American culture is almost devoid of meaningful rites of passage and rituals to transition boys and young males during different points in their lives, initiators are powerful developmental figures (Jolliff and Horne, 1999).

Mentors are real-life actors in the boy's life. They help him learn from others by being the skilled "master" to the protégé. In accepting the mentor's advice, learning to work collaboratively, and managing his emotions to fit successfully within social frameworks, the boy hones the tools necessary to fit into the world of work. It has been shown that the lack of positive mentoring hinders males' career and personal development (Horne et al., 1996).

Elders are those who hold a collective concern for the cultural context of any given community and educate the next generation into the ways to carry this culture forward. Elders are at Erikson's (1980) generative stage, giving back to the world through supporting and nurturing the younger generation. They help young males evolve into a greater sense of meaning-making, connection to others, and spiritual life. As elders "hold down the fort" culturally and spiritually, they make space for younger men to "experiment and stretch." They preserve the values of the community so that as the young men mature into healthy manhood, they can carry them on. Without elders, young males are lost; the same is true when young males are without true community (Horne et al., 1996).

FINAL THOUGHTS

The pathway to becoming a man is laden with challenges and developmental tasks that call into question the ways in which young boys and adolescents emerge into manhood. Traditional theories of male development chart a course with predictable life stages and passages as well as developmental homework that males must accomplish. They are aided by tribal, community, institutional, or national rituals and rites of passage that signal the successful transition from one stage to another.

Early childhood lays a foundation for trust and a sense of curiosity, will, and agency if the boy is raised in an environment in which caregiving is consistent, developmentally appropriate, and nurturing. At the transition to school age, children stretch their wings, take the first steps of separation from their parents, and—in the case of boys—begin casting off close ties to mother and all that is considered "feminine." Peers become the most important socializing agent and in order to join the "boy club," young males adopt behaviors and norms that are affirmed by the most powerful boys on the social ladder.

Adolescent boys are consumed with physiological changes, forming peer relationships, and charting an initial course toward adulthood. Unlike girls, they are thrust into individuation—separation from parents and community of origin and culture—earlier and more forcefully, as part of being a real man is being "independent." Yet most boys still long for connection, even as they move toward greater individuality. Finding and forming a positive peer group has powerful predictive value in determining emotional and psychological health and well-being, as well as a productive entry into adulthood. Adolescent males are more prone to risky behaviors than are girls, and media and other forms of socialization tend to glamorize risk-taking.

As masculinity is a cultural concept that is shaped by historical, economic, and political forces as well, boys are subject to reading the signs as to what constitutes being a real male in the society in which they grow up. With an increasing absence of fathers in the home, mentors in schools or the community, or traditional forms of apprenticeship in the workplace or military, they often struggle to find appropriate guidance. This leaves young men looking to the media or their peers for signs as to how to behave, what to think, and how to posture. The road to becoming a "real boy," many would argue, is harder to discern than ever, and developmental uncertainties leave many stumbling to find their way or lost by the waysides.

The new psychology of men movement has advanced different models of supporting boys and young males to achieve an expanded sense of masculinity and wholeness that translates into better mental and emotional health and well-being. It also challenges males to take on more family and communal responsibilities but recognizes that it will take a community of men—elders, mentors, role models, initiators, and nurturers—to make this a reality. In creating a network of men who can pave the way to positive masculinity, society could reverse some of the devastating effects of toxic masculinity and assist men, women, and children in forming healthier partnerships to affect not only this generation but those to come.

POINTS TO REMEMBER

- Traditional theories of male development are built on stage theories in which boys and men navigate distinct periods of life that hold developmental tasks that they must master in order to progress through the lifespan successfully.
- Boys suffer the effects of the boy code, which is based on four socially impressed tenets: Sturdy Oak; No Sissy Stuff; Give 'Em Hell; and Big Wheel.
- Boys and adolescent males are pushed into greater separation and individuation at earlier ages than are girls in order to prevent the effects of feminization and dependence, yet researchers have discovered that boys rely on friendships and connections as much as girls do but may express them differently.
- Boys need relationships as much as girls, but socialization to power and dominance hampers their ability to feel comfortable in the relational domain and some may even develop "relational dread."
- Boys and adolescent males need father figures, mentors, and role models, especially given the geographic and emotional absence of so many fathers; yet, there is a dearth of polestars available to help them on their journeys.
- The new psychology of men models places great value on traditions and relationships that lead boys to become "whole males." This includes taking a positive psychology approach to male development and looking at the ways in which other men can nurture healthy development at different stages of the boy's life.

Chapter Two

Failing to Make the Grade

How Boys Struggle to Succeed in School

Boys failing at school in larger numbers than girls is not new. It dates back to at least 1980 when the push for girl power and gender equality in education began (Tembon and Fort, 2008). At that time, girls were more likely to drop out of school than boys; however, recent data shows that approximately 7 percent, or 1,353,660, of males aged sixteen to twenty-four dropped out of school in 2016 as opposed to 5 percent, or 1,332,100, of females (Child Trends Databank, 2018; U.S. Census Bureau, 2017). To put this in perspective, in 2016 there were 19,338,000 males aged sixteen to twenty-four in high school (U.S. Census Bureau, 2017).

Some studies suggest the current high school dropout rate is related to concepts of masculinity that do not align with academic pursuits; yet, it remains true that boys fall behind in school at alarming rates and, if they do not catch up in the primary grades, they seldom ever do (Gove and Cvelich, 2011; Jha and Pouezevara, 2016). While many of the barriers to academic success fall outside of the classroom, there are specific strategies available to improve education within the classroom (Jha and Pouezevara, 2016). It is, therefore, necessary to understand how educators can help boys grow into academically strong men.

RESEARCH AND OUTCOMES

While boys benefit from relatable texts, male teachers, and single-sex classrooms, these simplistic solutions may inadvertently reinforce hegemonic masculinity, or the belief that men are dominant and women are subordinate

(Jewkes et al., 2015; Yavosky, Buchmann, and Miles, 2015). Yavosky et al. (2015) found that in high school males, the need to show masculinity overshadowed positive academic performance.

In recent studies, girls tend to show a greater affinity for citizenship behaviors such as organization, listening, effort, cooperation, and participation in school, leaving boys to struggle with academic performance (DiPrete and Buchmann, 2013). Noncognitive skills—those that are related to patterns of thought, behavior, and/or feelings, such as spending minimal time completing homework, lower grades, and grade retention—were also indicators that affected male students in negative ways (Borghans, Duckworth, Heckman, and Weel, 2008; DiPrete and Buchmann, 2013). Sommers (2013b) and DiPrete and Buchmann (2013) contend that boys benefit from active, hands-on learning and that "schools have become feminized spaces [that do not] accommodate boys' learning orientations" (Yavosky et al., 2015, p. 6).

The academic gender gap has occurred due to a belief by males that effort, attentiveness, studying, and hard work are feminine traits, rather than masculine; therefore, achievement becomes a more difficult endeavor (Jackson and Dempster, 2009; McGeown, Goodwin, Henderson, and Wright, 2012). School-aged boys face a dilemma; either they can practice the academic behaviors that lead to success or they can "distance themselves from feminized academic practices to the detriment of their school achievement" (Yavosky et al., 2015, p. 10).

Heyder and Kessels (2013) posit that there are both negative and positive masculine traits that have a direct effect on learning. Negative traits include being disconnected, a propensity toward violence, and "devaluing the feminine" (Yavosky et al., 2015, p. 1). These would clearly be of detriment to young men attempting to succeed in school. Positive masculine traits such as being competitive, showing leadership acumen, and rationality would be of benefit to the school-aged male (Heyder and Kessels, 2013).

Yavosky et al. (2015) found that masculine traits varied only slightly when considering race and socioeconomic status (SES). Some masculine traits could be found across all SES and, surprisingly, white young men were the most rigid in terms of "gender-typical behaviors" (Yavosky et al., 2015, p. 19). Interestingly, Hispanics and blacks were "most susceptible to the negative impacts of masculinity" (Yavosky et al., 2015, p. 20); yet, these same traits were responsible for an overall decline in grade point average. When these facts are translated into academic content areas, boys tend to excel in math while struggling in subjects such as English (Yavosky et al., 2015).

Other research shows that boys are less mature than girls at the age of five, when school traditionally begins (Newkirk, 2002; Reichert and Hawley, 2010). The average male is also less verbal, less socially mature, and more active than the average girl of the same age (Berk, 2017). Today, young boys are expected to learn to read in kindergarten. At this age they are not developmentally prepared for such a task, puting them at a distinct disadvantage (Kuper and Jacobs, 2019). A language-based classroom is the norm, yet research shows that girls are stronger in language at a younger age, putting boys once again behind young ladies in academics (Newkirk, 2002; Reichert and Hawley, 2010).

In yet other studies, boys from disadvantaged homes tend to fall behind even faster and are less prepared to take on the rigors of school (Guo, 2016). It turns out that "boys are more sensitive than girls to family disadvantages" (Guo, 2016, p. 2). Using siblings as the litmus test, boys were more likely to fall behind due to "poverty, mother's low education, bad neighborhood quality, and a slew of other factors" (Guo, 2016, p. 3). For all these reasons and more, male specific interventions must be considered.

INTERVENTIONS TO ADDRESS MALE ACADEMIC DISENGAGEMENT

With a clear understanding of the data and literature, it is important to also understand what educators can do to re-engage the male school-age population in meaningful academic pursuits. While some pundits refuse to acknowledge a difference between the learning styles of males and females, advocating for interventions and strategies that help increase the graduation rate of young men can have positive impacts on a nation, not just a single student.

A boy-friendly classroom environment must ensure safety and support whole-child, multisensory learning (Warble, 2018). Boys need to develop relationships with adults and peers, have experiences in which they collaborate with peers as well as times when they can be independent learners, have some choice and responsibility in their learning, and be challenged with complex tasks (Warble, 2018). In general, a classroom that engages boys might include more debates, games, and contests that "capitalize on the boys' spirit of competition" (Sommers, 2013a, p. 3).

Delaying Entrance to Kindergarten

Entrance to kindergarten is not required in every state across the United States, nor is there a consistent age to begin. Some states require students to be five years of age by September first, others by January first, and still others use July, August, or October. The discrepancy causes issues for children who could be as much as a full year older than their classmates. This continuum poses the biggest threat for boys as they mature at a much slower rate than their female counterparts. One option is to begin male students later, a trend seen by Dhuey, Figlio, Karbownik, and Roth (2017) in approximately 20 percent more affluent families. Boys who begin kindergarten at age seven show a "measurable advantage compared to younger classmates over the long term" (Samuels, 2017, n.p.). On average, the young male who begins school at a later age than his female peer is likely to have higher test scores, 2.1 percent more likely to attend college, and 15.4 percent less likely to commit a crime prior to sixteen years of age (Dhuey et al., 2017).

Praise and Positive Encouragement

Positive encouragement and praise are something that all children thrive on and boys especially respond to this strategy. Using rewards as often as possible instead of consequences, creates an environment where boys are more willing to work and succeed. Schools and classrooms that use Positive Behavioral Interventions and Supports (2019a) experience a decrease in distractibility, aggressive behaviors, and office discipline reports, while conversely they show "improvements in prosocial behaviors and emotion regulation" (Bradshaw, Waasdorp, and Leaf, 2012, p. e1144).

Supporting students in the classroom, educators should begin by explicitly teaching the expectations, creating a reward list as a whole group, and providing acknowledgment for appropriate actions (Positive Behavioral Interventions and Supports, 2019a). Using a proactive classroom approach, educators will find that management becomes easier and time on learning increases (Positive Behavioral Interventions and Supports, 2019a). Rewards can be anything that excites the child such as a few minutes of extra recess, earned time to play basketball with a friend and the PE teacher, helping in another classroom, using a special chair, or having a special someone (either school personnel or a family member) come share lunch. The rewards do not need to cost the educator money, although some choose to purchase pencils or other small items.

Male Mentors

Young men from black and Hispanic homes, "regardless of socio-economic background, are disproportionately at risk throughout their journey from their youngest years to college and career" (My Brother's Keeper Alliance and MENTOR: The National Mentoring Partnership, 2016, p. 4). While blacks and Hispanics are not the only young men who can benefit from mentoring, this single fact shows the need for male mentors who can create strong and meaningful bonds with young men who may be in danger of becoming a statistic later in life. Males who have mentors are more apt to have better "attitudes, motivation, social/relational skills, academic outcomes, and physical health" (My Brother's Keeper Alliance and MENTOR: The National Mentoring Partnership, 2016).

Addressing the deficits of the young male, the mentor will need training and continued professional development in order to understand and address the specific needs of the child. My Brother's Keeper Alliance and MENTOR: The National Mentoring Partnership (2016) offer an excellent program guide as well as benchmarks and enhancements for the "Elements of Effective Practice for Mentoring" (p. 32).

Boys as Active Learners

Young men need more time to play and engage in physical activities than their female counterparts. They need to move and have trouble when they are expected to sit still and listen. In one study girls were 19 percent less active than boys at age twelve (Telford, Telford, Olive, Cochrane, and Davey, 2016). A study by Swearer, Espelage, Vaillancourt, and Hymel (2010) found that boys become restless faster and tend to become aggressive when frustrated more often than female peers. Educators should create learning situations that involve movement and/or give boys more room to move (Ricks, n.d.). Examples include having small group learning on a rug instead of a table or at the very least, give boys a wobble chair (it looks like a mushroom but has a bowed bottom that swivels). Active learning includes structured competitive games, movement breaks, and a combination of teamwork and competition (Lahey, 2013).

Engaging Boys in Arts Education

Using the arts to engage boys in learning has a multitude of benefits, especially for students who struggle with traditional academics. Struggling students can "use the arts as an outlet through which they can demonstrate their own competence, genius, and exceptionality" (Warble, 2018, p. 66). According to Warble (2018), several of Gardner's learning styles are directly linked to arts education and offer many benefits for children that include:

- developing self-esteem
- acceptable ways to express emotions and feelings
- creating and understanding personal reality
- processing information in a unique way
- engaging students whose learning styles are more musical, kinesthetic, and visual
- encouraging innovation and creativity
- developing the skills of problem-solving and creative thinking
- supporting lifelong arts appreciation

Reducing Suspensions

In one study during the 2009–2010 school year, 3.3 million students were suspended, and black children were three times more likely than their peers to be suspended (Schott Foundation for Public Education, 2015). Another study indicated that 71 percent of all suspensions named boys as the culpable party (Ricks, n.d.). To reduce suspensions, educators and administrators should look at positive behavioral supports and interventions, social justice measures, and community service consequences as solutions (Positive Behavioral Supports and Interventions, 2019b; Jean and Rotas, 2019).

Recess as a Necessary Outlet

One of the worst things a teacher can do is take away recess to punish a male student. Students who had unstructured play time during the day received higher grades and were able to concentrate better than their restricted peers (Harvard University, 2015). Yet another study found that students who engaged in recess felt safer at school and increased time on learning (Robert Wood Johnson Foundation, 2012). While these studies did not differentiate between boys and girls, the assumption is that boys benefit from recess. Ricks (n.d.) offers solutions to punishment such as picking up ten pieces of trash or running a few laps prior to being allowed to join in recess fun.

Universal Design for Learning

This is a way of teaching that provides students with alternate learning and assessment opportunities as well as teaches to student strengths. It is based on scientific data that supports a variety of teaching and learning styles to accommodate student growth (CAST, 2019; Young, Jean, and Mead, 2018). Using a framework that includes why (engagement), what (representation), and how (action and expression), all learners can find a path to success (CAST, 2019).

Providing multiple means of engagement ensures that students are actively engaged in the work at hand; thereby creating purposeful and motivated learners (Young et al., 2018). Educators must find what specifically interests each student; minimizing distractions, preventing boredom through differentiated activities, fostering collaboration, promoting high expectations, and creating a reflective assessment are all important pieces of student engagement (CAST, 2019; Young et al., 2018).

Providing multiple means of representation speaks to the myriad ways in which students can present their understanding of new knowledge (Young et al., 2018). Educators promote this facet by presenting information both verbally and visually, highlighting information and ensuring schema is in place, as well as guiding the process of learning through clarification of information and support of learners (CAST, 2019; Young et al., 2018).

Providing multiple means of action/expression ensures that students are strategic and goal-directed (CAST, 2019). Educators must provide a plethora of tools, technology, and tiered supports to "guide, support, facilitate, and enhance" (Young et al., 2018, p. 103) students and enhance learning outcomes.

Hands-On Learning

At least one study suggests that while women prefer to work with others, men prefer to work with things (Su, Rounds, and Armstrong, 2009). Preschool children are most apt to engage in concrete learning and activities that require manipulatives (Warble, 2018). As boys have a natural propensity to take things apart and build things, class work at the elementary and middle school levels should include activities and final projects that engage students in the building or making of things (Sommers, 2013a). Creating video presentations, mechanical representations, and similar activities will engage young men in academics without their feeling feminized.

Some middle and high school courses should be geared to the hands-on approach such as wood shop, mechanics, graphic arts, and similar classes. Typical classes, such as English, may also have a hands-on twist as educators can create final assignments that are more in tune with individual student strengths. Massachusetts, for example, has a vibrant vocational-technical high school program in which students spend half their time in academic classrooms and half their time in a field placement (Sommers, 2013a).

One Massachusetts vocational school in particular is leading the way in launching struggling students—especially boys, many of whom come into the program with a fourth grade reading ability (Sommers, 2013a). These young men are subjected to college preparatory classes and an "intense, individualized remediation program until they read proficiently at grade level" (Sommers, 2013a, p. 5). The boys are willing to endure the struggle only because they look forward to the apprenticeship portion of the program (Sommers, 2013a).

Increasing Executive Function Skills

Organizational skills are usually not a young male's strong suit. To help boys complete assignments and turn them in, it is helpful to teach them an organizational system that limits forgetfulness. A sticky note on a desk with an ordered list and/or a divided notebook might help keep things moving in the right direction. If remembering the routine is an issue, students might benefit from a list on the board or posted on the table for when they enter the room in the morning. Teaching one step at a time limits confusion and reinforces the best behaviors (Vercelletto, 2016).

Equally difficult for boys is task persistence. Teachers and parents can set the tone by reminding students that they must finish what they begin (Vercelletto, 2016). Set a timer and instruct the student to work until the timer stops. Then offer a break prior to returning to the task at hand. This process shows the student he can succeed without feeling overwhelmed, thus building perseverance (Vercelletto, 2016).

Textbook Options

School textbooks are yet another source of gender information for students. Evans and Davies (2000) research analyzes traits pertaining to masculine and feminine stereotypes in elementary reading textbooks. While males were portrayed displaying both stereotypical masculine and feminine traits, there was not a significant crossover of traditional boundaries of masculinity (Evans and Davies, 2000). Overwhelmingly, females were emotionally expressive and passive, while males were "often portrayed as aggressive, argumentative, and competitive" (Evans and Davies, 2000, p. 268). Among male characters, masculine traits outnumbered feminine ones. This infrequency reiterates to boys that these feminine characteristics are not pertinent or important for masculine behavior; therefore, educators must find ways to integrate textbooks with suitable male role models, vocabulary that is gender neutral, as well as settings and subjects that appeal to boys of all sorts.

Teaching Boys to Love Literacy

Boys tend to struggle more with the acts of learning to read and reading itself as opposed to girls (Wong, 2018). A 2018 study from the U.S. Department of Education (McFarland et al., 2018) shows that at all three testing points, ages 9, 13, and 17, boys lag in reading as compared to their female peers. Beyond the fact that boys tend to be academically late bloomers, they spend less time processing, decoding, and are "more prone to skipping passages or entire sections [of books]" (Wong, 2018, n.p.). A 2009 Canadian report (Ministry of Education) offers the following strategies to teachers to help improve boys' literacy skills.

- choose appropriate resources
- allow time for socialization and talking
- provide regular breaks to read and write
- find positive role models to influence attitudes and beliefs
- teach to boys' learning styles
- introduce critical literacy skills

- include a variety of assessments
- use the arts to make literacy tangible
- find the relevancy for boys
- facilitate learning through technology
- include families in the process
- make literacy a school-wide focus
- use single-sex small groups as appropriate

Home-School Partnerships

Including families, especially the male figure of the family, in the equation to re-engage boys in the classroom is a much-needed step. When a family and educator bond and continually send a message to the student that going to and staying in school, working hard, and thinking deeply and creatively is important to their success, these children are more likely to succeed (Epstein, 2010; Young and Jean, 2018a).

Epstein (2010) created one of the first frameworks that defined six necessary elements of a well-formed partnership between family and school. These include (1) offering parenting advice and assistance, (2) two-way communication, (3) bringing families—especially the menfolk—into school to volunteer, (4) providing information on how to help with homework, (5) including families in organizations that advise and make decisions, and (6) collaborating with the community to provide resources, services, and activities to families (Epstein, 2010). Using these six keys as a starting point, schools and educators can begin to form relationships that become stronger over time and strengthen the education of all children, but especially the young boys and men in the classroom.

FINAL THOUGHTS

Boys and men are failing out of school, and life, at much higher rates than girls and women. Due in part to the 1980s push for girl power and equality, classrooms became feminized and teaching was geared, in part, to cater to the female student. With a multitude of factors to contend with, it is up to schools and educators to find ways in which they can connect with male students to turn back the drop-out rates both at the high school and college levels. Once educators begin to teach to all students using interventions and strategies that focus on a variety of learning styles and needs, male students will have a fighting chance to become active participants in the global economy.

POINTS TO REMEMBER

- The academic gender gap began prior to the 1980s and continues to this day. Black and Hispanic males are more likely to fail out of school than their female counterparts, yet all boys are susceptible to this failure.
- The feminization of school is one reason given for male academic failure. This belief that schools are geared toward how girls learn is confirmed through a variety of citizenship behaviors. Noncognitive behaviors all affect male academic success.
- Boys mature more slowly than girls; thus, expecting young men to perform at the same level academically, automatically sets them up for failure. In many cases, it may be advisable to have boys begin school a year later in age than girls.
- There are many interventions and strategies that can be put into place to ensure boys are successful in the classroom. Praise and positive encouragement, mentors, family partnership, and recess are a few of the nonacademic ways in which schools can help young men succeed.
- Educators who use universal design for learning, active and hands-on learning experiences, a focus on executive function skills—helping boys to love literacy—and arts education are more academic ways to ensure male success as they grow and graduate.

Chapter Three

Not an Easy Process

Navigating Race, Ethnicity, and Gender Identity

One of the major developmental tasks of adolescence is the formation of an identity that is unique to each individual and that helps launch the young person into adulthood with a secure sense of self. Erikson (1980) proposes that if this task is not successfully completed, the individual will be left in a state of confusion that can hamper success in many life areas. While some authors such as Arnett (2015) believe that contemporary individuals may not really reach the identity versus confusion stage until what he calls "emerging" or young adulthood, it is clear that the seeds of identity formation begin in infancy and continue through the emerging adult stage.

A positive sense of self is critical in so many ways as it affects one's self-esteem, sense of self-efficacy, career path, faith or spiritual development, interpersonal relationships, and mental health and well-being (Benson and Elder, 2011; Weir, 2017). The composite sense of self is profoundly influenced by component parts such as gender, racial, and ethnic identities that come together to make up each unique personality. How well these parts function as a whole deeply affects the ease with which young people navigate life transitions and make prosocial choices for themselves (Benson and Elder, 2011).

For some young people, the word "identity" is confounded by the fact that in late childhood and adolescence they are wrestling with the implications of having many different identities, comprised of gender identity, racial and ethnic identity, faith identity, and cultural identity and connection to community and family of origin (Benson and Elder, 2011). At times, these identities may come into conflict or may defy easy integration into a wholistic sense of self. That kaleidoscope of identity components must be explored as it relates to boys' and adolescent males' coming to a healthy sense of masculinity in contemporary America.

Comedian and author Michael Ian Black (2018) describes the problem of masculinity in his essay "The Boys are Not All Right." In it, he succinctly sums up the dilemma facing boys and young males:

> The past 50 years have redefined what it means to be female in America. Girls today are told that they can do anything, be anyone. They've absorbed the message: They're outperforming boys in school at every level. But it isn't just about performance. To be a girl today is to be the beneficiary of decades of conversation about the complexities of womanhood, its many forms and expressions. (n.p.)

Boys, though, have been left behind. No commensurate movement has emerged to help them navigate toward a full expression of their gender. It's no longer enough to "be a man"—as there is no clear definition of what that means.

MAJOR THEORIES OF IDENTITY FORMATION IN CHILDHOOD AND ADOLESCENCE

Erikson: Stage Theory

Erikson (1980) crafts one of the earliest stage theories that position identity development as a major task of the fifth stage of life. Erikson (1980) is the first to construct a theory of ego identity status and is generally credited with the term "identity crisis." In developmental terms, a "crisis" denotes a turning point in which an individual must move one way or the other in terms of his development; in particular, if he was not able to master the developmental task of that particular stage successfully, development in subsequent stages would be compromised (Erikson, 1980).

Erikson's (1980) Identity vs. Role Confusion is the fifth stage in this lifespan schema. Taking place roughly at adolescence, this stage requires necessary consolidation of a tentative first adult identity in order for the adolescent to move forward with confidence into the work of crafting a career and finding intimate relationships. Community, Erikson (1980) points out, is critical in helping the young man negotiate this stage, as it requires him to draw from previous learning and synthesize that knowledge into useful application to his newly constructed role.

Marcia: Identity Status Theory

Marcia (1966; 1980) defines the developmental task of identity achievement as exploring and eventually making a commitment to an identity that is multifaceted in that it is tailored from many life aspects such as career, friendships and relationships with others, faith, political and civic engagement, gender and ethnic identities, and sense of purpose in life. This model of identity development includes four different identity statuses to include identity diffusion; identity foreclosure; moratorium; and achievement (Marcia, 1966). The primary work on identity development is located in adolescence; however, identity development really is a lifelong process that begins in infancy.

Marcia's (1980) work mainly focuses on the early adolescent period and involves the two processes of exploration and commitment. These two categories describe the young individual's movement toward a consolidated sense of self that had goodness of fit for him or her. Exploration is defined as active thinking, exploring, and comparing possible identity components with what one knows about oneself (Marcia, 1980). This can be aided by specific curriculum, career exploration opportunities, mentorship, and parenting that encourages young people to think about their strengths, proclivities, and what paths might serve them well in the world of work and in contributions to society as a whole (Marcia, 1980). When committed to a role, a career path, or an ideology, the individual can move forward with a clear sense of purpose toward his future; this includes a sense of educational planning, values, career path choices, secondary and post-secondary academic curriculum, and experiences that can enhance this choice (Marcia, 1980).

According to Marcia (1966; 1980) students in the moratorium stage are actively engaged in exploration of their identity but have not yet made a commitment to a consolidated identity; they are at risk of floundering without having a variety of opportunities to try out and develop skills and interests before they arrive at a consolidated choice. This is where guided career exploration, vocational curriculum, mentoring, and job shadowing, as well as service learning experiences become extremely valuable. Students in the achievement stage have made their initial choice and that choice is an informed one because they have had the aforementioned experiences (Marcia, 1980).

Those in the diffusion stage are either not exploring because they do not have opportunities or are not able to come to a commitment (Marcia, 1980). This may occur more frequently with youth who come from lower socioeconomic status backgrounds, poorer school districts, or communities with fewer resources. In such cases, the breadth of experiences available to their more privileged peers may be severely restricted, depriving them of the chance to test out different ideas and paths. Diffusion is the direct result of a young person's avoidance of the exploration and commitment processes, and this indecision, for the most part, comes with a good deal of anxiety, as he knows that he is supposed to come to resolution in order to be able to move forward with a well-constructed path that fits his interests and personality (Marcia, 1980).

Students who fall into the foreclosure category have come to identity choices that are premature because they have not had the benefit of properly exploring what might be available to them in different venues or they may have been limited in their ability to experiment with various identities (Marcia, 1966; 1980). This may happen because of external pressures from family, culture, religion, or financial exigencies. The societal impress can have a heavy influence on what identities and career paths boys and adolescent males deem acceptable, and parents may deliberately or inadvertently reinforce gendered identity stereotypes (Marcia, 1980).

In some cultures, identity is almost destined at birth, based on such issues as social class, caste, or color, while in others, parents and communities may pressure children to choose certain academic concentrations or career paths such as business and finance because it is believed that these provide economic security (Sankaran, Sekerdej, and von Hecker, 2017). Gendered concepts of masculinity also may be passed down or reinforced, even if they do not necessarily fit the individual male's profile (Marks, Bun, and McHale, 2009). Several examples include:

- A young male who is discouraged from entering a "female" profession
- . A boy who is told that he is expected to be the primary economic provider to his family, therefore, he should not choose a "risky" profession like the arts
- An adolescent in a military family or in a family-run business who may be pressured to carry on the tradition, whether he is interested or not

If an individual has been able to encounter and resolve his identity crisis, he is said to be at the stage of identity achievement, which is characterized by an internalized sense of self, rather than one that is defined by external factors (Marcia, 1966; 1980). If it had "goodness of fit" for the individual, he is infused with a sense of energy moving forward into young or emerging adulthood confident of being on a pathway that will lead to personal satisfaction and contributions to the larger society.

Rice and Dolgin and Brown and Knowles: Acquiring Self-Esteem and Self-Actualization

Developing self-esteem is integrally related to identity consolidation. Rice and Dolgin (2005) identified six perceptions that the pre-adolescent continuously reflects upon and that have a substantial influence on self-esteem: (1) who I really am; (2) who I think I am; (3) who others think I am; (4) who I think others think I am; (5) who I think I will become; and (6) who I think others want me to become.

Brown and Knowles (2007) also add that the degree to which preadolescents and adolescents experience positive self-esteem is dependent upon four factors: (1) the amount of perceived control they have over situations around them; (2) their level of acceptance by others whom they hold in high regard;

(3) the degree of competence they exhibit in undertakings; and (4) their sense that they are "virtuous" with others.

Identity formation, according to Brown and Knowles (2007) is in full bloom and young adolescents seek to find aspects of personality that are consonant with their sense of self. This phase is best understood in terms of Erikson's (1980) Identity vs. Role Confusion stage where young adolescents desperately want to belong to a social group, yet they still quest for individuality. Acceptance by the desired social group provides a sense of personal validation. This group membership helps them begin the transition away from family of origin and permits them to try on different aspects of self (Brown and Knowles, 2007).

Baxter Magolda: Theory of Self-Authorship

Baxter Magolda's (2008) identity development theory centers on the concept of self-authorship. This concept is defined as an individual's ability to find within himself the source of definitions of his beliefs, values, identity, and social relationships (Baxter Magolda, 2008). This internal ability answers three salient life questions (1) How do I know? (2) Who Am I? (3) How do I want to construct relationships with others?

Baxter Magolda (2008) describes identity formation as a journey toward self-authorship that when achieved, means that the individual can write the story of his own life; however, there are four stages or phases that lead to such internal confidence and identity consolidation. The first phase is called "following formulas" and involves external sources defining the individual; these sources are usually family of origin, community of origin, faith community, and cultural mandates, which have a powerful impress on most young people (Baxter Magolda, 2008). For boys, media and other outer sources suggest to them what it means to be a male in this society and what kinds of identities are safe to adopt.

The second phase is called the "crossroads." At the crossroads, the previous formulas no longer seem to suit the individual so well and the need for new plans arises. This is a point of psychological discomfort or outright crisis, as if the individual were wearing a suit of clothing that no longer fits (Baxter Magolda, 2008). This is often caused by life changes or transitions, such as going off to college or leaving the family of origin, but the crisis also may occur more slowly and in more subtle ways. The key indicator is dissatisfaction with self and discomfort with the structures built previously (Baxter Magolda, 2008).

If the individual can successfully navigate the crossroads and life work, he can move into the third phase of "becoming the author of one's life." Here, the individual creates an environment in which he is free to choose his own beliefs, value systems, and ways of being in the world (Baxter Magolda,

2008). He also is confident enough in himself to stand up for these if he encounters opposition. The final and fourth phase of this model is called the "internal foundation" because it is here that the individual is firmly grounded in an authentically derived sense of self that is wholistic and has goodness of fit (Baxter Magolda, 2008). The individual is confident in who he is and forms relationships that are freely chosen with others who are capable of true intimacy and mutuality (Baxter Magolda, 2008).

Higgins: Self-Discrepancy Theory

Higgins's (1987) self-discrepancy theory is a departure from most identity theories in that it shies away from a focus on the individual and focuses instead on discrepancies between three "self-domains" and two "standpoints" of the self. The three self-domains are the actual self, the ideal self, and the "ought" self (Higgins, 1987). The actual self is how the individual or other people see a person's attributes or characteristics, the ideal self is comprised of attributes or characteristics that the individual or other significant people wish he possessed, while the "ought" self is what the individual or others believe he ought to possess (Higgins, 1987). In this model, both the individual and outside forces (such as parents, teachers, friends, or society) play a powerful role in self-assessment.

When there is a discrepancy between what is and what should be, whether from the individual or outside forces' view, there is resulting disappointment, dissatisfaction, or even shame or embarrassment (Higgins, 1987). When there is consonance between and among these, there is a sense of consolidation or wholeness in that the individual and those who matter to him affirm that his character meets standards, both internal and external. With consonance, there is a sense of pride and self-efficacy, whereas with discrepancy, there can be many negative emotional outcomes (Higgins, 1987).

Some discrepancy is inevitable during adolescence, as the young person develops his identity, and Higgins (1987) suggests that there are strategies that can help to relieve negative emotional states during this challenging time. In terms of young males' development, it is easy to see how there could be discrepancies between socially constructed and affirmed definitions of masculinity (toughness, physical prowess, emotional detachment) and the true nature of many boys (Higgins, 1987). These discrepancies can lead boys who do not subscribe to the boy code to have less than positive self-images.

Markus and Nurius: Possible Selves Theory

Possible selves theory is one of the newest and most interesting theories in the "Self Family" of psychology studies in that it aims to comprehend individuals' behavior through the concept of "possible selves" (Markus and Nurius, 1986). The theory posits that possible selves are a representation of all the components of the self-concept that an individual might become, desires to become, or fears becoming (Markus and Nurius, 1986). Possible selves have been termed a road map for individual behavior. Oyserman, Bybee, Terry, and Hart-Johnson (2004) describe research that correlates an increased number of positive possible selves with a reduction in risky behavior, such as substance abuse or sexual activity.

Sun and Shek (2010) demonstrate in their work that teenagers are less likely to take part in problem behavior if they can conceptualize possible selves that have meaning and purpose for them. Helping young males envision positive, attainable possible selves that fill them with a sense of direction and vitality can cut down on risk factors that can undermine academic, social, and personal achievement and well-being.

COMING TO A CONSOLIDATION OF RACIAL AND ETHNIC IDENTITY

Holcomb-McCoy (2005), like many other researchers, believe that race and ethnicity play important roles in the identity development of minority youth. The task of identity formation in the racial and ethnic spheres most often falls to adolescence, although the consolidation of identity doesn't necessarily end as one transitions from that period. Ethnic and racial identity consolidation does not end until the young person makes a firm commitment to his identity (Holcomb-McCoy, 2005).

The preteen, teen, and even emerging adult years most often are marked by exploration, examination of the aspects of ethnic and racial identity inherited from family of origin and community culture, and then move into active exploration to see what, if anything, one has inherited that has any meaning to the young person's emerging sense of self (Holcomb-McCoy, 2005). As Gay (1994) points out, the concept of forming a sense of identity is more difficult for minority students, as they have developmental work to do individually and culturally.

Racial Identity

Derman-Sparks (2012) outlines the development of racial and cultural identity and attitudes in stages that begins in infancy when babies gradually become aware of themselves as separate beings and are subtly influenced by the cultural identity reflected in their daily interactions, their home, and their care. At about six months old, children begin to notice and respond to skin color cues—for example, the skin color of their primary caregiver—and throughout their first and second years, they are primarily influenced by the cultural content of their families. If these children are also in daycare, they might be influenced by the cultural connections between home and school (Derman-Sparks, 2012).

The socializing context of home continues when they are three and four years old with language development, cultural ways of being, and gender norms reinforced in the family and extended family's daily life. At this age children are not yet attuned to gender and racial identity constancy and are also able to absorb societal stereotypes, which in some cases may lead to questioning, fears, and discomfort around differences (Derman-Sparks, 2012). At this early age, children show evidence of being affected in terms of self or group identity due to others' messages about whether they are superior or inferior.

In the age period from five to six, children of homes that differ from dominant or mainstream culture may experience what Derman-Sparks (2012) calls a "bicultural crisis" when they enter school. They may handle this crisis by assimilating into the dominant culture, remaining connected to home culture, or learning to move back and forth between the two. Despite the fact that some children in this age range choose to identify only with "their own" or may even use prejudicial name-calling when angry or aggressive, they are at a ripe age for developing critical thinking skills and social justice attitudes around issues of difference (Derman-Sparks, 2012).

By the time children have reached middle childhood, children of color are aware of bias against their own racial or cultural group and may show the psychological effects of internalized racism. It is during third grade when many children are said to drop out of school psychologically due to a rise in discrimination, name-calling, and rejection due to race, gender, class, disability, or sexual orientation. While children at this time can critically think about and be empathic to those who are subject to negative stereotyping, those of minority and marginalized groups have a harder time forming positive identities than those of the majority (Derman-Sparks, 2012).

While there are some who believe that after the age of nine children's racial attitudes tend to stay constant unless they go through some sort of life-changing experience, others believe that attitudes are fluid and can be influenced by relationships, education, and aspects such as travel (Derman-Sparks, 2012). By the time children reach early adolescence, they are interested in learning more about their own cultural group and role models, are aware of differences between perspectives of diverse cultures, and are attuned to disparities between how significant adults talk about and act about discrimination and racial issues (Derman-Sparks, 2012).

During adolescence, there is a focus on the reworking of individual and group identity; this process can go in different directions. They may reclaim their identity, heritage, and history; adopt the majority culture; adopt a "color-blind" stance; navigate a bicultural existence between home and school;

identify primarily with others of the same ethnic and racial background; or struggle among various identities and their demands (Derman-Sparks, 2012).

There are several prominent models of racial identity formation and they share several similarities. Cross (1971; 1991) proposes a model that is comprised of five stages and adopts the concept of "nigrescence" or becoming black, as the foundation. Later, Cross and Fhagen-Smith (2001) developed a life span model that moves from infancy and early childhood through healthy black identity. The authors discuss the influences of high race salience, low race salience, and internalized racism as they play into the formation of a sense of self in relation to race. Cross's model is now called the "People of Color Racial Identity Model" (Cross and Fhagen-Smith, 2001).

Social identity theory tells us that our identity is founded in the emotional and psychological significance and the level of value that an individual derives from membership in certain social groups. Two facets—the attachment that the individual feels in relation to the group and the level of importance he places on membership in it—are how one identifies socially (Cross, 1991). When related to racial identity, two concepts—centrality and private regard—come into play (Cross, 1991).

Centrality describes how important the concept of race is to an individual because not all blacks see their race as being equally important to their identity. This is what Cross (1991) means by high or low race salience. Private regard refers to whether an individual holds a view of his race in a positive or negative light. In cases in which an individual has experienced and internalized the negative impact of racism, his private regard of being black is probably quite low (Cross, 1971; 1991).

While there is not a vast cache of research on gender identity among black males, much of it is centered on the degree of conformity to socially reinforced gender-typed beliefs such as hyper masculinity or other cultural stereotypes such as athlete, performer, or adventurer (Collazo, 2016; Dancy, 2007). Existing research and literature indicate that some boys and adolescents invest heavily in socially reinforced gender types while others feel comfortable in deviating from them (Collazo, 2016; Dancy, 2007). As with racial and ethnic identity, gender identity depends upon centrality and private regard in relation to how much importance a boy puts on gender and how positively or negatively he views male group membership.

The social identity model of racial identity is valuable in that it provides a snapshot of individuals' variation in racial identity at a particular point in time, but it does not give the developmental perspective that other models such as Cross's (1991) and Phinney's (1993) stage models do. These models begin with individuals in basically "unexamined" stages of racial identity, with either little awareness or awareness formed through families, social networks, and other socializing factors.

As boys develop in the social-cognitive domain, social group norms and expectations become more powerful, and broadening social experiences, such as entering secondary school, take place, adolescent males begin to explore and question their racial identity, seeking out more information and asking questions of significant others (Holcomb-McCoy, 2005). This occurs at a time when they are most likely questioning other aspects of identity as well.

If adolescents and emerging adults have positive experiences in their active exploration, receive support and information, and engage in education that encourages them to explore, discuss, and reflect upon their heritage, then they can move forward into a healthy, achieved, or committed racial identity in which that component is viewed as an important, positive aspect of the self. Both racial centrality or high race salience and private regard coalesce into a sense of self and self-esteem (Holcomb-McCoy, 2005).

MODELS OF ETHNIC IDENTITY DEVELOPMENT

Ferdman and Gallegos (2001) propose a model of Latino cultural identity in which racial identity is a secondary identity in the Latino culture and the model hinges on six orientations that are a process, rather than a stage model. This model can range from Latino-Integrated to White-Identified, representing a wide range of identities; for example, some Latinos, the authors found, may identify as white or claim a color-blind status (called undifferentiated) in which they either view racial identification as nonexistent or as unimportant (Ferdman and Gallegos, 2001). White-Identified Latinos adopt the values and cultural beliefs of whites, adopting the majority culture as their sole reference for identity.

Latino-Integrated individuals see the larger society in terms of race and identify with Latino culture and its values, feeling a part of the Latino rather than the majority culture (Ferdman and Gallegos, 2001). Latino-Identified have a more dualistic view of both race and social identity, viewing race as fluid and society as a dualistic construction of race and ethnicity (Ferdman and Gallegos, 2001).

Ferdman and Gallegos (2001) also describe Subgroup-Identified Latinos as those who have a strong identification with a specific subgroup of Latino culture; such individuals see other subgroups as subordinate to their own. There also is an orientation of "Latino as other" by which no stake in any specific subgroup is held by the individual; the authors believe that this is often due to lack of knowledge or uncertainty about one's actual heritage (Ferdman and Gallegos, 2001).

Identity Formation among Young Latinos

Sanchez, Chaney, Manuel, and Remedios (2018) set out to study the function of gender role attitudes as they relate to ethnic identity development in Latina/o preadolescent youth. The researchers were particularly interested in how familial ethnic socialization influences ethnic identity development and how young people's cultural and ecological contexts play roles in this formation. This concept posits that family is a powerful force at the core of theoretical formulation of children's identity development and ethnic socialization (Sanchez et al., 2018). For young males, the two gender role attitudes (machismo and marianismo) lay at the intersection of familial ethnic socialization and ethnic identity development.

Sanchez et al. (2018) note that the family unit has been seen as the primary ethnic socializing agent through the passing down of cultural values, socially acceptable behaviors, and attitudes about one's ethnicity. This occurs both overtly (direct actions by which parents teach children about their ethnicity) and covert socialization, which occurs when parents transmit cultural values in less direct ways, such as preferring to continue to speak their native language at home, having cultural objects in the home, eating traditional foods, listening to ethnic music, or weaving aspects of one's culture into everyday life in subtle ways.

The authors report that existing research demonstrates that family ethnic socialization affects Latino youth's identity development in positive ways that persist over time; for example, among Mexican-origin secondary school students, high familial ethnic socialization when students were in middle school led to an increase in their ethnic identity exploration and resolution in high school (Sanchez et al., 2018). Among those who received positive familial ethnic socialization in fifth grade, their positive ethnic identity and pride were seen in middle school.

There is some evidence that Latino adolescent males and females may experience familial ethnic socialization and the development of ethnic identity in different ways (Sanchez et al., 2018). Girls were more greatly influenced by family socialization and ethnic identity exploration and resolution than were Latino boys (Sanchez et al., 2018). This is possibly due to the expectation that Latinas will remain closer to their family and will be the agents of socialization of the next generation. When families invested time in overt and covert socialization of boys to their heritage, they helped to promote positive ethnic identity resolution among their sons (Sanchez et al., 2018).

As boys transition to adolescence, there is a greater emphasis on gender role socialization; this means that boys become much more cognizant of family expectations about what appropriate male roles are and what masculinity means within any given culture. Castillo, Perez, Castillo, and Ghosheh (2010) point out that many Latino families are rather traditional in their view of gender and believe that there are distinctly different gender role expectations for women and men. The culturally relevant construct of machismo comes into play when considering gender-role socialization of Latino boys and adolescents. Sanchez et al. (2018) describes two operationalized expressions of machismo: (a) traditional machismo, which is a focus on Latino men's independence, dominance over women, and hypermasculinity and (b) caballerismo, which is a focus on more positive aspects of masculinity such as social responsibility, protection of the family, and emotional connectedness.

Studies link traditional machismo gender role attitudes with poor mental health outcomes for males, including experiencing anxiety, depression, and stress (Castillo et al., 2010; Sanchez et al., 2018). Emotional disconnection is another negative health outcome; yet, boys and adolescents whose families stress caballerismo appear to benefit from positive affiliation, academic attitudes, and higher educational goals (Castillo et al., 2010). Latino boys who are raised to be nurturing, responsible men and fathers remain closer with their families of origin and develop a stronger sense of purpose, connection to their culture, positive ethnic identity resolution, and the belief that they should be intimately involved in their marriages and child rearing (Castillo et al., 2010). Sanchez et al.'s (2018) work illustrates the importance of family socialization for both positive ethnic identity development and the avoidance of negative health and well-being outcomes related to toxic masculinity.

Asian American Identity Development

Kim (1981) developed a model of Asian American identity development through which individuals may enter and exit during different periods of development. Ethnic awareness rises out of one's family structure, which is a powerful influence in Asian American identify formation; such awareness forms prior to integration of peers and school culture. Yet, as with Ferdman and Gallegos's (2001) model, there also may be white identification among Asian Americans in which individuals opt to identify with and assimilate into white culture to avoid difference or discrimination (Kim, 1981).

Kim (1981) posits that many Asian Americans may be "awakened" to sociopolitical consciousness; this frequently occurs with adolescents and emerging adults as they begin to understand the inherent links between racial and ethnic inequalities and acts of discrimination and the political and economic structures of the country. In many cases, young Asian Americans seek out and join forces with others who fight oppression and discrimination and they may become more politically active in the search for a more just society.

Asian American youth also may be redirected to a sense of pride in their heritage and culture; this is bolstered by significant others who share this pride, such as families, social networks, and Asian American cultural organizations (Kim, 1981). If they incorporate these positive attributes into their sense of self, they develop a healthy identity that allows them to interact with and appreciate others of diverse cultures.

American Indian Identity Formation

"Native American identity is multifaceted," wrote Horse (2005), a Kiowa scholar. "Many issues or elements (such as ethnic nomenclature, racial attitudes, the legal and political status of American Indian nations and American Indian people, cultural change, and one's sensibility about what being a Native American means in today's society) influence native American identity" (Horse, 2005, p. 62). American Indian identity, Horse (2005) believes, is highly personal in its formation and relates to one's experiences as an American Indian or as a member of a tribe, as well as how one views oneself. Identity is also influenced by whether or not one is part of a group of people who share common ethics, which can give one a sense of "collective consciousness" as well as an individual identity (Horse, 2005).

Horse (2005) shares five important factors that shaped American Indian identity formation. The first factor is the degree to which one is grounded in their American Indian culture and language. This is dependent upon the cultural transmission, usually from family and tribal community, and it can be threatened when young men are forced to live in majority cultures, sent to school off the reservation, or grow up in settings in which there are negative stereotypes about American Indians in general (Horse, 2005).

The second factor is the validity of personal genealogy (whether that person is officially recognized as a member of a certain tribe), and a third is the membership in or lack of membership in a tribe (Horse, 2005). Subscribing to what are the traditional pillars of American Indian belief structures and values, such as spirituality and being in balance and harmony with the earth and the natural world, is also important to identity formation and is the fourth factor (Horse, 2005).

Finally, a young man's self-concept as an American Indian also plays a role. Like many other racial and ethnic groups in this country, American Indians frequently find themselves juggling multiple identities, yet there is a uniqueness to their identity formation in that they have a worldview unlike any other because they are the only people indigenous to this country (Horse, 2005).

Garrett (1996) offers another model that proposes four different levels of acculturation into mainstream society. The first is the traditional identity in which American Indian youth operate within the traditional sphere, speaking, thinking, acting, and practicing only the traditional cultural beliefs, language, and customs (Garrett, 1996). Other youth may be marginal in that they can speak and interact with both native and dominant cultures but do not fully identify with either. This is the second level of acculturation and leaves them in a kind of cultural limbo, unable to fully assimilate in either world.

Bicultural American Indians, who encompass the third level of acculturation, can generally fit into mainstream society; however, they are able to embrace their cultural heritage and its values and beliefs. They can navigate both cultures, giving them a "dual citizenship" of sorts (Garrett, 1996). Finally, bicultural American Indians are assimilated because they embrace only the values, culture, and language of mainstream society, divorcing themselves from the heritage of their ancestors (Garrett, 1996).

Brown and Smirles (2003) examine the bicultural ethnic identity of American Indian adolescents. The authors found that such youth have a distinct challenge in that they must learn to live and thrive in two cultural environments that are distinctly different from one another. Because identity formation and its search are at a peak during adolescence, these teenagers were found to have struggles with developing a bicultural identity (Brown and Smirles, 2003).

Since individuals can identify equally with more than one cultural group, this process is far more complex than the formation process for mainstream or dominant culture youth. This is even more complex because of the "existence of multiple tribes, distinct cultural areas, different languages, degree of Indian blood lineage, intertribal and interracial marriages, and the experience of living in two worlds" (Moran and Fleming, 1999, cited in Brown and Smirles, 2003, p. 9) that American Indian adolescents experience.

The researchers found that American Indian teenagers who lived in tribal states had stronger tribal exploration than those residing in non-tribal states, probably because there were more cultural activities and stronger group identity through participation in those activities and events (Brown and Smirles, 2003; Horse, 2005). Those youth living outside of tribal areas still had strong identification with their tribal background, but "their overall identity may suffer due to their lack of ability to explore their tribal culture" (Brown and Smirles, 2003, p. 17). Those who had experienced stereotyping had a stronger tribal identity; the authors suggest that this is consistent with Phinney's (2003) research that proposes that those who experience discrimination in some form are more likely to explore their ethnicity in a deeper fashion.

Herring (1999) wrote that,

> helping Native American Indian and Alaska Native male youth can be very challenging. Achievement of the separation from the biological family and the development of an independent identity are complicated by factors such as experiences of oppression and discrimination, low socioeconomic status (SES), limited access to publicly funded services, as well as the consequences of these factors. (p. 117)

Herring (1999) notes the incredible diversity among families, customs, traditions, and language, rejecting the common stereotypes of homogeneity in these populations. Many Natives who had the ability to "pass" as being part of the majority culture or who could pass as another ethnicity voluntarily chose to do so.

In addition to the typical developmental crises of boyhood and adolescence, Native males experience their own set of identity issues, beginning with the fact that 60 percent of them are genetically mixed, leading to conflicts among who is pure Indian and what that means (Horse, 2005). Some Native males are pressured to assimilate, while others are caught between home and school cultures. In part, identity crises relate to the degree of family culturation.

Traditional families are tied to culture of origin and fight to preserve that culture; transitional families choose to live within the majority culture yet still may retain some vestiges of traditional culture. Bicultural families most often speak the languages of both cultures and adhere to some cultural aspects of each without fully accepting one over the other; assimilated families have left their traditional ties behind to fully blend into majority culture (Winters, 2015).

Herring (1999) points out that traditional Native boys have learned most of the skills that they need for adulthood by the time they have reached age ten. They are given tremendous freedom, learn by observing older males, and gravitate toward the toys that teach them hunting and warfare abilities at an early age. Most rites of passage into adulthood begin with childhood's end at age ten in which they are prepared for the fuller range of adult male skills. Culturally, boys are steeped in the oral tradition, in-the-present time orientation, cooperation, spirituality, and living in harmony with, rather than trying to dominate, nature (Herring, 1999). These attitudes and beliefs often place them in direct contrast to mainstream culture.

According to Herring (1999), suicide is the second leading cause of death among Native males, who have the highest rate of completed suicides. Alcohol, depression, isolation, and loneliness are also problems among young Native males, particularly if they are separated from the tribe and sent to majority schools or if they experience intergenerational conflicts due to disagreements about culturation (Winters, 2015). Among those who opt to "pass," there are struggles with answering the question of who they really are in terms of identity. Horse (2005) mentions that a common frustration among multicultural youth is that they are singled out with questions about their identity.

One further stress on Native identity formation is that intertribal individuals, who have roots in several different tribes, must choose in which tribe they will enroll (U.S. Department of the Interior, n.d.). The choice can have huge political, economic, and cultural results. This is exacerbated if Native individuals marry into other racial groups. In all, identity formation for those who have been affected by colonialism is a complex process. Some Native youth will choose to respond to past and current history and politics by deliberately returning to their tribal roots, others will choose assimilation, while still others struggle with the need to form and consolidate their identity.

Identity Development among Immigrant Youth

Schwartz and Petrova (2018) studied identity development among immigrant youth, noting that cultural identity and personal identity are bound together for our nation's immigrants. How easy the process of identity formation during adolescence and emerging adulthood becomes is a function of many factors. The first aspect is that of ethnic identity, and the authors note that the need for such an identification within a particular immigrant group seems to be related to the degree to which that group is perceived to be culturally different from the dominant culture of the nation (Schwartz and Petrova, 2018). For immigrant youth from those groups seen as most different from the majority, therefore, there is a tendency to place value on developing a common identity among themselves.

This is also true for groups that are most stigmatized or perceived to be threats to the dominant culture. This is being experienced by Muslim and Mexican youth, for example, at the present time in the United States. Some immigrant groups—those seen to be most European in feature and culture—are embraced more readily than those who are seen to be foreign or dangerous (Waters and Pineau, 2015). Those young people who are rejected by their host nations require particular creativity in forming a positive cultural identity. Young male immigrants who are not of European descent may be doubly handicapped in forming a positive identity given that they must be aware and abide by both majority culture and that of their own heritage group (Waters and Pineau, 2015).

Spurgeon and Paredes (2012) found significant differences in the lived experiences of adolescents based upon their family of origin and their ethnic identity; for example, those from Asian and Latin backgrounds tended to be more committed to family loyalty and the perceived necessity of caring and providing for family members. While these were viewed as positive traits, they interfered with young people's ability to engage fully in their studies or in extracurricular activities that competed with family responsibilities.

In times of mass immigration and where there are large immigrant groups united by a common culture and language, the greatest backlash occurs. This is reflected in public perceptions and statements suggesting that "our country" is being overrun or invaded by immigrants, or that immigrants are here to steal jobs and benefits. Spurgeon and Paredes (2012) concur, suggesting that there are both realistic and symbolic ways of stereotyping immigrants.

Immigrant youth from groups labeled negatively may hide their identity or try to be stealthy or "pass" in the face of such hostile reception.

Schwartz and Petrova (2018) believe that since ethnic and national identity facilitate personal identity, those from groups that are discriminated against may have their personal identities constrained or damaged, affecting both psychological and physical health and well-being. This study, like others, finds that biculturalism is the most adaptive of identities in that bicultural individuals affirm both their ethnic and their national identities (Schwartz and Petrova, 2018). If avenues to doing both are blocked, however, young people's sense of self and self-esteem can be harmed and arriving at a truly consolidated positive identity can be hampered.

Arriving at a positive ethnic identity is critical for all ethnic groups. Ethnic identity is described as an individual's sense of belonging, involvement, and self-identification with the culture and social practices of a group. Various studies (Borrero and Yeh, 2011; Phinney and Ong, 2007; Romero and Roberts, 2003) have linked this positive ethnic identity to good mental health, psychological well-being, self-esteem, prosocial tendencies, academic performance, and resilience.

GENDER IDENTITY

The literature on gender identity taking place in preadolescence and adolescence is meager. Models of gender identity development historically have centered on early childhood and the identification and behavioral choices of children (Early Childhood National Centers and the National Center on Parent, Family, and Community Engagement, n.d.; Ghosh, 2015). These include studies of such variables as when children first identify themselves by gender, how they associate with gendered activities, and what role parenting may play in their identity choices (Early Childhood National Centers and the National Center on Parent, Family, and Community Engagement, n.d.).

The gender intensification hypothesis of Hill and Lynch (1983), however, postulates that the physical, emotional, and social changes that adolescence bring with them provide a heightened awareness of and interest in gender. This awareness includes what it means to belong to a certain gender membership, whether or not one fits his assigned gender, and what he feels about that. There is a dearth of research examining whether gender identity centrality and private regard are like racial identity, in that they increase in interest and intensity during adolescence, or whether one takes precedence over the other (Rogers, Scott, and Way, 2014).

More measures of the possible intersectionality of these variables are needed. Young blacks who positively evaluate their racial group have higher self-esteem and fewer depressive symptoms (Santos, Galligan, Pahlke, and

Fabes, 2011). Those who have stronger ties to their racial group are higher achievers in school. In other words, young males who have the strongest connection with their racial group fare better in school and have more positive self-esteem. There is a parallel when it comes to gender identity. Santos et al. (2011) found that African American young males who have less rigid gender beliefs are more engaged with school and are higher achievers.

Kroger (2007) notes that early adolescence is a period during which boys are most apt to start coming to terms with their sexual identity because of the biological changes that puberty brings with it. The sexual self of the early adolescent is conceptualized in three different ways: (1) sexual or gender identity; (2) sex or gender role; and (3) one's sexual orientation (Kroger, 2007). Personal identity is rooted in feelings of being male, female, androgynous, or undifferentiated.

Roles, on the other hand, are derived from the ways in which an individual chooses to express his or her biological gender when with others; that expression is governed by social norms and stereotypes about appropriate behavior in particular settings (Jean and Buckley, 2019). Adolescents also become more aware of who they are attracted to; yet, they may experience angst if those objects of attraction transgress social or cultural norms.

Growing up Gay, Transgender, or Gender Fluid

To grow up as a boy who does not conform to typical definitions of masculinity is to find the pathway to identity littered with challenges. Understanding gay identity development is critical for parents, educators, and anyone interested in boys' and young males' development. To date, a vast majority of the research on this topic utilizes quantitative methodologies, so the stories of this process, from an "insider's" vantage point, have been largely missing.

More recently, there have been studies that invited gay and transgender students to speak to their own experiences and developmental processes (Thoreson, 2016). Cass (1979; 1984) is credited as being the source of the earliest model—a stage process—for understanding the identity development of gay men. This model posits that there are developmental tasks inherent in each stage that must be successfully resolved in order to move progressively toward a more integrated and authentic sense of self (Cass, 1979; 1984).

Cass's (1984) first stage of gay identity development is identity confusion—a stage during which the individual compares and contrasts what he knows about being gay with his own thoughts and behaviors. This period of introspection leads to a personalization of the information about gayness and, most often, the individual has to confront the question of whether he believes he is actually homosexual or not. Unless one has had real-life connections to other gay individuals, his concept of being gay is a socially derived one, usually tinged with negative connotations (Cass, 1984). This level of consciousness conflicts with the previously internalized view of oneself as a heterosexual, throwing the individual into identity confusion (Cass, 1979).

This conflict within the individual can be extremely upsetting and difficult to process, especially in instances in which the young person feels isolated. There are many possible outcomes to the initial identity questioning to include rejecting the concept that one is gay; learning more about his identity through counseling, reading, or researching; or reaching out to others to learn about their experiences (Cass, 1984). In some cases, individuals vehemently reject this possible identity and instead identify with homophobic individuals and their behaviors (Cass, 1979). Successful resolution of this stage is critical to healthy identity consolidation.

Identity Comparison, Cass's (1979) second stage, is characterized by a point in development where an individual has accepted the fact that he might be gay. With that acceptance, the individual now must face the consequences of identifying this way; without an open and supportive network of people around him, the young person may become socially isolated and withdraw from those he feels will not accept who he really is. This also is a point at which a gay young person may begin to feel the effects of heterosexual privilege; it is a time of potential psychological risk for depression, anxiety, and other maladaptive symptoms (Cass, 1984).

If he experiences a lack of supportive gay role models and heightened pressures to conform to heterosexual norms, or if the individual is harassed or bullied, he may retreat further into a covert world (Sue, 2010). He may feel forced to present as heterosexual to maintain friends, social status, or family acceptance. Presenting in social situations with the opposite sex, avoiding exchanges of information that are personal in nature, and masking dress or actions that may be labeled as homosexual are all ways that young people may hide their true identity; however, this covert operation exacts a heavy toll on many boys and young men (Cass, 1979).

In the third of Cass's (1979) stages—identity tolerance—gay youth move toward a tolerance of their identification. This may also come as a result of not being able to find acceptable ways of masking or coping with denial of who they truly are. Cass (1984) notes that social support becomes salient, and if there are not family members or friends who can lend this support, a young gay male might begin to look into community groups, support groups, gay bars, and other places to explore the gay community.

While in previous stages he might have been resistant to doing so, now the individual may identify with and seek out gay peers. But that community must be found in places where the young man feels safe, accepted, and socially adept. It is the goal, as stage three closes, for the individual to be able to comfortably commit to the homosexual identity; however, this commitment might be expressed only to one's self or a small group of gay peers (Cass, 1979).

In the fourth stage of identity acceptance, the young male understands and embraces his gay identity in more concrete ways (Cass, 1979). Of note is the fact that this is generally when a young gay individual seeks out and cultivates gay interpersonal relationships through building small networks of people whom he can trust. With them, he comes to realize that there is no significant deviance and disappointment with his gay identity. Previous confusions about identity and belonging clarify within this stage; however, at the same time, and given the increase in his connection to gay social supports, the individual realizes the incongruence between the gay community and the heterosexual community (Cass, 1979).

Recognizing this disparity, the individual may begin to feel conflicted about his relationships from previous stages of development (Cass, 1979). An individual might limit or outright ban the contact he has with those heterosexual relationships that cannot support his newly declared sexual orientation. During this stage, he may become more active in gay support groups, gay bars, gay events, and other gay specific activities to further explore and understand his identity and gain acceptance, as identity consolidation is borne of such positive interactions (Cass, 1984).

During the stage of identity pride, an individual is faced with the understanding they accept their gay identity and the heterosexual community rejects this (Cass, 1979). It is this lack of support from the heterosexual community that continues to lay the framework for some disruption, but the individual fights against this by adding support from the gay community. The emergence of the gay identity allows an individual to call upon the gay community for support and acceptance.

It is during this stage that an individual identifies not only as homosexual, but part of the gay community (Cass, 1979). This is significant because an individual validates his pride with a group of people with whom he can rely on when others in society reject them. A greater sense of community exists as an individual moves from feeling isolated and alone to identifying with the gay community. Shifting from peers and families who do not accept the homosexuality identity will emerge and an individual will begin to distance himself from these relationships to further facilitate a greater sense of support and community (Cass, 1979).

As an individual enters into stage six, he rejects his previous concerns about the heterosexual community as always being a threat to his identity and is able to differentiate supporters from nonsupporters so that he can maintain or create heterosexual relationships that positively feed his health and well-being (Cass, 1979). This can occur because now the young male is evolved to the point of recognizing that his sexual identification is only one part of who he is. In the presence of positive relationships and communities, he may be able to heal from previous conditions such as anxiety and depression.

In addition to Cass (1979; 1984), there are several other models for gay identity formation that include Fassinger and Miller's (1996) model in which a person may experience four stages (awareness, exploration, deepening/ commitment, and internalization/synthesis). This model is like Cass's (1979) model in that it addresses individual identity consolidation through interactions intra- and inter-personally. Worthington, Savoy, Dillon, and Vernalia (2002) propose five statuses that move from unexplored commitment (assuming that heterosexuality is the norm) to active exploration to diffusion which, if resolved, leads to a deepened commitment and finally synthesis of sexual orientation into a larger sense of the unique self. Unfortunately, all the models mentioned are fairly old and do not spend a great deal of time on other variables such as race, ethnicity, religion, or social class in considering whether or not there are universal stages of gay identity development.

In addition to these variables, researchers need to take into consideration ecological factors in identity formation. Environmental factors are critical to understanding how gay identity formation takes place. These environmental factors might include one's geography and culture, social network including parents, siblings, and other extended family, connection within the community, school ecology, and historical events that are not explicated in these gay identity models.

Gay identity development is significantly harder than heterosexual identity development because of discrimination, prejudice, and outright violence within contemporary society. Gay adolescents and young men must process their thoughts and feelings in the face of such challenges, and many struggle with a unique challenge of coming out in families who lack empathy, education, and knowledge of gay identity development. In the absence of positive gay role models and mentors, too many young males are left to problem solve these identity issues alone (Sue, 2010). They may feel shame and stigma, keeping their struggle deeply hidden.

Identity foreclosure is also critical to an understanding of identity formation, particularly for marginalized groups. This occurs when young individuals commit to an identity without the requisite reflection and self-scrutiny that an identity crisis brings about. In the absence of such a crisis, the young person adopts the values and ideals represented by their family and the culture around them. Konik and Stewart (2004) remark on the importance of exploration in gay identity formation since in its absence, young males may merely adopt identities that are expected by their families and dominant society rather than accepting who they really are.

Looking through the lens of trauma, an individual going through his specific stages may have an immense amount of grief, lack of support, and rejection from families, friends, and others in the community. As an individual passes through these stages, he suffers an overwhelming amount of information, thoughts, and feelings to further process his identity (National Resource Center for Mental Health Promotion and Youth Violence Prevention, n.d.). An individual has a significant amount of fear and shame attached to his identity in the early stages of his development; therefore, is it difficult to seek out support and guidance from others.

A major difference between heterosexual and homosexual identity development is the construct of homosexual individuals who are required to navigate their identity in a heterosexual world. Heterosexual individuals do not interface navigating their identity in a homosexual world. This has a major social implication that gay individuals already have a barrier in their identity development as they are self-identified as the minority. Socially, anything that deviates from the social norm is typically unacceptable (Levy, 2009).

One of the few qualitative studies of identity development in transgender and gender nonconforming youth was conducted by Katz-Wise et al. (2017). The researchers discovered several important themes in this process that they describe as complex and an interplay of both internal and external processes. Both young people and their families were interviewed and depict transgender identity processes that are both immediate and slow to unfold, including transitions (Katz-Wise et al., 2017). Many recall very early verbal and behavioral cues and appearance-based preferences; these include statements such as knowing that one was not his or her sex assigned at birth, choosing toys or activities that were associated with the opposite sex, or wanting to wear clothing or other accessories or styles related to the opposite sex (Katz-Wise et al., 2017).

Many interviewees and their families had feelings of dissatisfaction or levels of discomfort with their sex-linked physiology at very early ages, while others note that puberty, with its body changes, seemed to trigger transgender identification (Katz-Wise et al., 2017). Some parents of transgender children said that identification was clear in early childhood, but others came to their identification more gradually, over time (Katz-Wise et al., 2017). Those who were gender nonconforming recall not fitting into the binary system when young and described their resistance to this system as intentional, rather than merely a confused response to societal norms.

The interviewees often expressed the internal process of transgender identity development through external appearances such as adopting clothing or fashion styles associated with the other sex; yet many preferred to "pass," especially during adolescence (Katz-Wise et al., 2017). Also important to the participants was the point at which they wanted to be addressed with correct pronouns and names as they transitioned to their affirmed gender identity (Katz-Wise et al., 2017). When friends, family, and teachers did so, they felt respected and accepted—essential components of consolidating their sense of self.

When interviewees were able to receive social support and resources that affirmed their gender identity, they were able to transition and consolidate a true sense of self in ways that built their resiliency and well-being (Katz-Wise et al., 2017). Support included interactions with family, school, specialized groups, other transgender youth and families, and professionals such as counselors. The most important aspect they cited was safe spaces in which they felt free to talk about their experiences. In general, the researchers found that caregivers (immediate family) were most influential in transgender identity formation (Katz-Wise et al., 2017). A barrier to positive identity formation among nonheterosexual boys and young men is the violence to which they are often subjected by their peers and others.

Identity formation amid homophobia

A barrier to positive identity formation among nonheterosexual boys and young men is the violence to which they are often subjected by their peers and others. Lang (2018) writes that a decade ago, we became concerned as a society about the skyrocketing rate of bullying of queer and transgender students that led to a rash of suicides, but anti-LGBTQ+ harassment and physical violence is increasing even since then. McKay, Lindquist, and Misra (2017) studied twenty years' worth of data and prepared a meta-analysis of their findings, which were disturbing because while it might seem that young people today are more accepting and welcoming of the LGBTQ+ community, McKay et al. (2017) found that targeting and harassment of these populations has not improved in the last three decades. Some types of victimization, such as cyberbullying, appear to have worsened.

All these acts of violence have the potential to cause serious, long-term negative effects on the health and well-being of LGBTQ+ youth and adults. McKay et al. (2017) studied seventy-three thousand LGBTQ+ young people and found rates of school bullying to be at a record high. They combed more than twenty years' worth of data and discovered that LGBTQ+ students are two to three times more likely than their peers to be the victims of harassment, targeting, and bullying when in school (Lang, 2018).

Spurgeon and Paredes (2012) note that gay adolescent boys are often victimized and are at elevated risk for depression and mental health issues because of this. Boys are socialized to resist help-seeking behaviors; therefore, their risk of increased mental health problems is great, and suicide or suicidal ideation is not unusual. This, coupled with greater familiarity with and access to firearms, makes victimized boys and adolescent males more successful than girls in actually completing a suicide attempt (Spurgeon and Paredes, 2012).

In studies by Liu (2016) and Dwedar (2016) statistics indicate that LGBTQ+ high school students were three times more likely to be victimized than were their straight classmates. LGBTQ+ students routinely felt emotionally distressed at school because of factors such as hearing the word "gay" used pejoratively against them or being physically confronted, taunted, or made to feel unsafe while in school.

Warella, Rideout, Montague, Beaudoin-Ryan, and Lauricella (2016) produced a survey that revealed shocking figures—81 percent of transsexual youth reported having been sexually harassed in school, while the figure was 72 percent for lesbians. More than two-thirds of gay and bisexual adolescents said they had suffered sexual harassment at the hands of classmates; and even middle school students (22%) were harassed due to their gender identity or their sexual orientation (19%) (Warella et al., 2016). Such statistics indicate that identity formation for sexual minority boys and adolescent males is a perilous journey.

A 2014 survey revealed that 55 percent of LGBTQ+ youth experienced the feeling of being "unsafe" in their schools due to their sexual orientation, while three-quarters of all trans students reported feeling uncomfortable in class (Kosciw, Greytak, Giga, Vilenas, and Danischeswski, 2015). LGBTQ+ students were found to be likely targets of bullying or harassment (91%) and three times more vulnerable to sexual assault (Kosciw et al., 2015).

In 2004, Wyss conducted a study and interviewed gender nonconforming students in secondary schools in the United States. For students who began high school with an established sense of their gender identity, torment and violence by classmates was a regular part of their school experience (Wyss, 2004). Enduring these conditions negatively impacted their physical, emotional, and mental health and well-being, as well as inducing feelings of shame, lower self-esteem, and anger (Wyss, 2004).

Katz-Wise et al. (2017) confirm these findings, stating that for many transgender and gender nonconforming youth, school was the place in which rather than education, stigma, torment, and marginalization occurred. Many interviewees related being deliberately called by the incorrect pronoun or singled out for punishment for such things as going into the "wrong" bathroom or displaying affection to a partner (Katz-Wise et al., 2017). Active exclusion often took the place of bullying with some but almost every interviewee described systemic harassment related to their identity development processes (Katz-Wise et al., 2017). The already difficult process of coming to identity consolidation in adolescence was made exponentially more difficult when students did not feel embraced by their school communities.

Immigrant youth

There is a dearth of research on identity formation of immigrant youth, although estimates are that worldwide there are 258 million immigrants, with 36 million of them under the age of twenty, and almost 60 million in the United States (United Nations, 2017). Maynard, Vaughn, Salas-Wright, and Vaughn (2016) report that school-aged immigrant youth struggle with the assimilation process and identity formation, citing many of the same reasons that were described in other sections on ethnic identity formation. This struggle is also linked to varying definitions of "maleness" and "masculinity" derived from the homeland when they came into conflict with those of mainstream American culture (Maynard et al., 2016).

Identity formation of immigrant youth is also complicated by their susceptibility to bullying and victimization, like struggles mentioned earlier with other populations such as gay and transgender youth (Maynard et al., 2016). Immigrant youth are more likely to be targeted if they come from ethnic, racial, or religious groups that are viewed as outside of the norm of cultural acceptance, such as Muslims or Jews, who are harassed more than immigrants who are white or Christian (BRYCS, 2011).

School demographics play a role in the incidences of bullying and victimization of immigrant students (BRYCS, 2011). In more culturally and ethnically diverse schools there is a greater likelihood that immigrant students experience the feeling of being vulnerable or being perceived as different. In a school climate that deliberately celebrates diversity in all aspects of human identity, the process of identity formation and consolidation is made easier for those who are not from the majority culture (BRYCS, 2011).

ACADEMIC IDENTITY OF MINORITY BOYS

Today, no one debates the fact that in the United States African American and Latino boys and adolescent males are failing academically, including in standardized testing, graduation rates, and college attendance after graduation (Musu-Gillette et al., 2017). Latino males suffer the highest drop-out rates of any ethnic group in this country, and while the reasons for this differ among researchers, identity formation explanations hold sway among almost all theories (Musu-Gillette et al., 2017). For young males of color, social threats, problems with cultural assimilation, and the effects of institutionalized racism can interfere with their healthy identity formation (Osborne and Jones, 2011).

The concept of academic identity formation plays a powerful role in academic achievement disparities. Described as a sense of self derived from academic performance, sense of belonging in a school community, achievement, and academic engagement, academic identity appears to be in scant supply for ethnic minority males, especially those in high-poverty, urban schools (Matthews, Banerjee, and Lauerman, 2014; Osborne and Jones, 2011).

When students do not identify with their schooling, their motivation and achievement suffer; disidentification and disengagement have been described as the disconnection between self-esteem and academic performance and lie at the heart of the academic underachievement of ethnic minority males (Matthews et al., 2014). Educational practices within schools impinge upon positive identity development, motivation to achieve academically, and performance itself; these include factors such as low expectations for their performance, higher incidence of disciplinary action against them, and higher rates of placement in remedial and special education settings, and many male students are seen by teachers through an "oppositional antagonistic" lens (López, Ehly, and Garcia-Vazquez, 2002).

Minority males may suffer even more greatly from the developmental drop-offs in interest and motivation that accompany many young adolescents (Lee, 2008). If discouraged or disparaged or disconnected from the life of the school community, marginalized young men may turn to identities that are at odds with school values or may develop stress in the face of poor coping reactions to their marginalization. Lee (2008) describes identity development and academic identity development more broadly than many researchers, characterizing learning as a self-system that is comprised of many different aspects of the self that are displayed differently across cultural communities.

In this vein, Wright (2011) reports of ethnic minority males as constructing racial and academic identities under conditions that are complex and often conflicted. Those African American adolescent males who were academically successful, for example, managed simultaneously to both identify with their peers (belonging) while also having a strong, internalized sense of their own efficacy (Wright, 2011). High-achieving Puerto Rican secondary students were connected to their school through relationships with their teachers, but also held strong ethnic identities and developed social supports through extracurricular activities (Wright, 2011).

Matthews et al. (2014) suggest a much more multidimensional way of thinking about identify formation among minority males, for example, by asking the question: What influences the academic identity of a minority male student who possesses clear potential and skill but who is turned off from engaging with the school community due to factors such as discrimination, bullying, or marginalization? Academic identity, Matthews et al. (2014) argue, is made up of both social and personal dimensions that have a profound impact on academic achievement, engagement, and motivation.

The first dimension is made up of evaluation, which is the regard with which the boy holds his social identity and membership of certain groups (Matthews et al., 2014). This can result in feelings of satisfaction, shame, or pride. The second is importance, or the degree of value that he puts on a particular identity (Matthews et al., 2014). It is possible, for example, for an identity to be evaluated positively but not held in as high importance as another identity—such as evaluating one's identity as a student positively but one's identity as a football player as more important.

A third component of academic identity is that of attachment or interconnection (Matthews et al., 2014). This is an emotional appraisal of the boy's desire to belong, his bond with the school community, and his connection to peers and teachers. Obviously, when a sense of attachment is strong in these domains, his likelihood of school achievement and persistence to graduation increases (Matthews et al., 2014).

Behavioral involvement is a fourth component comprising one's commitment to taking part in actions that reinforce a group's status (Matthews et al., 2014). In the academic realm, this relates to self-regulation and self-direction, such as taking part in goal-setting, self-regulated learning, and self-assessment within the educational sphere. Doing these things regularly increases one's self-efficacy because, as each act of self-regulated learning and goal setting leads the boy to experience success, he is more likely to do those things again out of the belief that he will be successful; these successes, in turn, feed his positive self-esteem and willingness to remain engaged in the academic process.

Younger boys, Matthews et al. (2014) writes, are more likely to overestimate their academic abilities; as they progress through secondary school, they may suffer declines in their academic self-concept, self-efficacy, and willingness to engage if they encounter failures that shake their beliefs in their ability to be successful. At each stage of transition—from elementary to middle school, and then from middle school to secondary school—urban males are more likely to become alienated due to poor experiences in their schooling (Jensen, 2009; Matthews et al., 2014). This is exacerbated by the fact that the stakes continue to rise and the results of academic failure weigh even more heavily on their futures (Jensen, 2009).

Early high school—especially the transition from eighth to ninth grade—is when stakes are higher, social supports decline, and negative academic feedback becomes more damaging. This is the critical point at which schools must marshal resources to combat urban males' alienation, feelings of failure, and disengagement—which for many means exiting the school system altogether (Jensen, 2009).

The study reveals several academic identity types among minority males to include highly engaged and the severely disengaged as the most prominent (Matthews et al., 2014). Highly engaged students displayed all the characteristics of academically successful students to include self-direction; goal setting; connection to the school community; valuing academic success; and seeing the relationship between academic success and future achievement (Matthews et al., 2014). They experience personal pride and satisfaction and feel high levels of self-efficacy; these emotions fuel continued academic effort even in the face of challenge.

On the opposite end of the spectrum, the severely disengaged (or calloused poor) do not perceive school to be important and see the expenditure of academic effort as futile (Matthews et al., 2014). They are alienated from their peers and teachers within the school community and have low pride and self-efficacy. Because they do not value academics, their self-esteem is rooted in activities other than academic achievement. Because these students are only 16 percent of the entire sample, the authors challenge the prevailing notion that disengagement or disidentification attitudes are at the heart of academic underachievement among urban ethnic males (Matthews et al., 2014).

Matthews et al. (2014) found another typology in their study: the "sensitive-poor" student. These males differ in that they scored only moderately low on the identity dimensions and that they felt a sense of contrition for how poorly they were performing in school (Matthews et al., 2014). As students, they present a conflicted profile—on one hand they do not believe school to be important and they are disengaged from the school experience; yet, on the other hand, they do not disidentify from school totally (Matthews et al., 2014). These male students recognize that success in school is related to their personal evaluation, in that they realize that such achievement related to their sense of pride and competence. School success, it is clear, is linked to an internal sense of self-worth and self-respect.

Because of these emotions, such males are excellent candidates for interventions that could redeem their academic failures and provide that sense of personal satisfaction currently missing (Matthews et al., 2014). They can become more connected to their school communities if they reengage academically and socially. Unlike the severely disengaged, these students, with the right programming and relationships, can reap success and consolidate positive academic identities once again.

The authors found yet another category of academic identity, that of the "dispirited-connectors." Sadly, these students experience a sense of low academic self-efficacy, even though they exhibit a high sense of school connectedness and regard for academic success. These males display above average self-regulatory skills and are strategic thinkers. Given their profile, these students ought to be successful in school; however, they do not see themselves as capable of achieving their academic goals and completing their schoolwork successfully and therefore fail (Matthews et al., 2014). Such males are in conflict—they are overwhelmed by the academic tasks at hand but still are connected to their school, teachers, and peers.

This group holds much promise if teachers and other social supports can encourage them to persist, if they can be taught more effective academic skills and strategies, and if they begin to change their concept of self-efficacy over time through repeated successes (Matthews et al., 2014). Given males' help-seeking behaviors and avoidance of discussing emotions such as feeling overwhelmed or incompetent, however, they are at risk for not receiving the academic support that they need. Often, their teachers and counselors may be unaware of how deep their struggles are or may mistake their false confidence as competence or their avoidance of help-seeking as a sign that things are fine (Matthews et al., 2014).

Interestingly, the study also points to identity issues even among high-achieving male students (Matthews et al., 2014). These "model" students were found to be under a great deal of internal and external pressure to succeed and despite their high academic performance, they suffer from concerns about being able to maintain high levels of performance; this leads them to what the authors call "self-handicapping" or other defensive behaviors (Matthews et al., 2014).

They tend to cope poorly when they fail because since they hold academic success in such high regard, their sense of self-worth is damaged if they do not achieve (Matthews et al., 2014). Despite their high levels of functioning, they suffer more greatly in the areas of pride and self-worth if they do not meet lofty standards, and this can lead to emotional stress, anxiety, depression, or diminished well-being.

Moderate students showed the lowest frequency of self-handicapping behaviors and the best chance for well-being, given that they are strong academic achievers but have balanced qualities and other ways of deriving self-worth (Matthews et al., 2014). They hold the key to good psychological health and well-being in that they do not define themselves based solely on the academic arena. This allows them to disconnect a sense of self from academic performance. Even though they perform as well as model students statistically, the moderate males appear able to formulate an identity that is more well-rounded and is not dependent upon one variable, thus providing a safety net psychologically if they encounter an academically challenging situation (Matthews et al., 2014).

The results of Matthews et al.'s (2014) study stress the importance of academic identity formation as a particularly important, yet difficult, task of adolescence. For minority or marginalized males, this is territory fraught with danger and marks the place where many, especially urban African American and Hispanic young men, do not survive. These students then are often forced to seek out alternative identities that may contain elements of toxic masculinity or that, at the very least, set them on a course of underachievement, financial stress, social marginalization, and poor health outcomes (Matthews et al., 2014).

BUILDING ASSETS

It is important to look for solutions in the face of the daunting difficulties that so many young men encounter when forming positive identities. Groups who do well share some similar attributes. Remembering Matthews et al.'s (2014) "moderate" students of color, a model for success and well-being can be emulated. These young men knew the value of school, were hard workers, and experienced a positive sense of self-efficacy because of their efforts; however, their sense of self-worth is not intimately bound to being successful in the academic sphere. Young males who have multiple identities and involvement in things that matter to them and from which they garner satisfaction and pride fare far better, probably due to their ability to transfer positive attributes from those activities to their academic lives. Such involvement in religious groups, service activities, and strong family connections bolster their sense of well-being.

In writing on transgender identity development, Testa, Jiminez, and Rankin (2014) discover that having both the awareness of other transgender people and having engagement with them prior to identifying as trans is beneficial to their mental health and well-being. Awareness and engagement with others like them is particularly valuable if they occur at an early age such as childhood (Testa et al., 2014). Educational programs for children and adolescents that provide information about gender identity as well as representation of the transgender community in various media are ways that young people learn about and accept this designation prior to necessarily identifying themselves (Testa et al., 2014).

Testa et al. (2014) cite studies by others that indicate factors building resilience among trans individuals to include "the ability to define their own identity, a strong sense of self-worth, being aware of oppression, connection with a supportive community, and being able to cultivate hope for the future" (p. 33). The authors also reference a study of transgender people of color, finding six factors held in common that build resilience including: (1) having pride in their gender and racial identity; (2) being able to negotiate oppression; (3) positive family relationships; (4) health care and financial resources; (5) connections with an activist trans community of color; and (6) spirituality and a feeling of optimism for one's future.

Noguera (2008) remarks on the importance of the role of faith organizations and community mentoring programs in the lives of African American boys, as these affirm positive identity, promote pride, and ingrain a sense of responsibility for oneself and one's community. This is also found among high-achieving Latinos where family ties and cultural pride are sources of self-worth. Having a low regard for school success most likely protects them from failures and makes them more likely to persist even in the face of failure since their sense of self-worth is less tied to academics; however, it would be wonderful to add academic success to the list of assets for African American and Latino boys. Specific strategies could enhance the likelihood of school as being one more pillar of resiliency among minority males.

Knight (2015) writes about the common tropes associated with boys and young men of color; they are seen as violent, drug-involved, gangsters, hustlers, angry, withdrawn, or emotionally detached. These males are so culturally stereotyped that it is easy to fail to look beyond the negative images created (Knight, 2015). These young men, according to Knight (2015), engender feelings of threat among those who come in their presence. Few black and Latino teens, Knight (2015) found, feel like full and equal citizens compared to white peers.

When considering the theories of self-discrepancy and possible selves, one can see that there are practical implications of both. Skillful support systems can help young males reduce self-discrepancies and point out the many possible expressions of self-definition available to them. This sense of possibility is enhanced by fostering exploration in safe venues, remembering that most young males will not be drawn to typical talk therapy approaches; yet might be more likely to participate in self-exploration (Knight, 2015). Given that having a sense of purpose and finding avenues of self-definition that have meaning for the individual are foundations of well-being, there is great value in helping young males identify what holds internal meaning for them.

In Knight's (2015) research, black and Latino males in middle and high school in Boston were interviewed. A central theme among the interviews was the importance of relationships to these young men; many had family responsibilities or cared for younger siblings while their parents worked, and students described always being "on guard" at school due to their race/ethnicity and gendered stereotypes (Knight, 2015). When confronted with problems, they turned to trusted friends to share emotions, seek advice, and solve problems. Knight (2015) terms the boys' awareness of how they were viewed stereotypically and their attempts to disprove negative stereotypes as "emotional complexity," admiring the strengths that they displayed.

For Knight (2015), a simple solution to some of the disengagement and poor academic performance of young males of color is to acknowledge their complexity and assets and build upon them. Emotions that run deep—such as love and family loyalty—counter the common negative tropes. Knight (2015) offers George Jackson Academy (an all-male school in New York) as an example in which middle school students engage in a curriculum to develop a more loving ethic.

The culminating activity of the curriculum is for each boy to complete a project that demonstrates his love for someone he did not usually show love to but who was beloved by him (Knight, 2015). Usually family members, these designees receive various selfless acts that aim to connect boys with their own humanity and often-ignored part of their identity. Rather than reinforcing the cultural expectations that boys and young men are distanced from their emotions, this school challenges the stereotype boldly, giving boys who are silent often for fear of victimization or who do not have people in their lives to discuss emotional issues, an opportunity to publicly claim that part of their being (Knight, 2015). Nurturing capacities that lie in each boy through different curricula like this one is a way to fight the boy code head on (Kastner, 2018).

Gilpin and Proulx (2018) provide many lesson plans, links, and resources that can be used to engender reflection and discussion about what it means to be a man in contemporary society. The prompts provided take on both definitions of masculinity and toxic masculinity and help us think about ways to create positive masculinity that benefit both men and women.

Spielberg (1999) writes that our society doesn't provide "avenues of constructive and heroic identity formation for a great number of young men" (p. 25). This is particularly true among the economic underclass who are virtually shut out of the global economy. While he argues for continued parental support and encouragement as boys and young men individuate, he also believes that young males need "objects of devotion"—other groups and attachments beyond their extended family (Spielberg, 1999). These groups can be religious, cultural, athletic, service-oriented, or any orientation if they provide constructive forums for identity formation.

Spielberg (1999) discusses the necessity of "systems of meaning" that are embedded in such groups; these are the broad, unchanging value bases that "guide behavior and help people find solace when facing the difficulties of life" (p. 31). Too many contemporary young men are bereft of such systems and their normal developmental needs, such as connection to others, commitment to a cause, and expression of their unique selves in all domains (including creative and spiritual) fall by the wayside.

These systems of meaning provide "purpose, clear values, and opportunities to feel effective and in control" (Spielberg, 1999, p. 31). Among Spielberg's (1999) ideas are national conscription for a year or two to either public service or the military, school-based mentoring programs, youth employment programs, school scholarships, and other activities that provide for meaningful contact with positive adults and activities that contribute to one's school, community, or larger society.

FINAL THOUGHTS

Identity formation and consolidation is a multifaceted process that encompasses all domains of human development. A salient aspect of adolescence, identity formation requires the individual to move from a set of more externally derived components to those that are more internal in nature and spring from the uniqueness of each individual. In late childhood and "transescence" (Eichhorn, 1968), boys become caught up in the process of trying to figure out the masculine code and compare and contrast themselves to the dictates of that code.

Finding out and coming to grips with what it means to be a male in this society is difficult work. That work is made even more complex for boys and adolescent males who fall outside of the majority mainstream guidelines for masculinity. Factors such as race, ethnicity, religion, and sexual orientation all play a role in how the young man pieces together a sense of self-in-the-world. For those who are of minority cultures or marginalized in other ways, it can be difficult to locate positive images of masculinity that challenge toxic manhood. Role models and mentors portraying positive and healthy masculinity are essential in young men's lives.

So, too, are family, community, and school. There are myriad ways to support healthy identity development among boys and adolescent males that increase the chances of prosocial behavior, academic and career path success, and physical, emotional, and relational well-being. It takes a societal awareness and the willingness to act in the face of existing practices, stereotypes, and cultural mandates involving masculinity to lessen the burden of being a contemporary boy in the United States. Moving from "machismo" to "caballerismo" in all segments of society will take a concerted effort if we are to help young males reach that ideal of social responsibility, emotional connectedness, and family engagement in their lifetimes and with a legacy to pass on to the next generation of men.

POINTS TO REMEMBER

- Identity formation is a salient task of adolescence that involves resolving crises that are personal, sexual, career, spiritual, and academic in nature.
- Boys and young males struggle to consolidate an identity that is true to the unique self in the face of societal messages about what it means to be "a man."
- Youth who are members of minority or marginalized groups have a more difficult process of coming to a healthy consolidated sense of self.
- There are several models of ethnic and racial identity formation. Each presents varying degrees of acculturation to mainstream society, ranging from remaining true to ethnic roots to being "bicultural" to assimilating.
- For transgender and gender nonconforming youth, the complex process of forming an identity that is consistent with their own sense of self is facilitated best by acceptance and support from immediate family, as well as schools, support groups, and professional support.
- As all boys and young males go through the process of identity development, they benefit from the positive support and interactions with family, older male role models and mentors, community and faith groups, service projects, and opportunities to explore career paths through hands-on experiences.

Chapter Four

Nurturing Nice Guys

Parenting to Support Prosocial Behavior in Boys

Parenting all children, but perhaps especially boys, has become more complex than ever. Elium and Elium (2004) write about the core issue with boys as being that:

> they lack consistent, kind, and firm leaders with rules that make sense. Because we are so busy trying to "make it" financially or trying to "find ourselves," we have delegated the parenting of our sons to the institutions of culture, and we are suffering because of it. . . . We are too familiar with the effects on our sons of growing up too fast in a technological age. Yet instead of leading them firmly by the hand into manhood, we are leaving the job to day-care workers, teachers in overcrowded classrooms, TV writers, movie and rock stars, gangs, the neighbors, and sometimes even the courts, juvenile hall, and probation officers. Parenting is harder today than it used to be.

The effects of contemporary parenting of boys can be seen in a kind of "male vulnerability," as Krugman (1995) calls it. Contemporary males, he feels, are becoming increasingly vocal about the stress and strain of being socialized to be a real male—meaning a tendency toward social and emotional isolation, often accompanied by compulsive patterns of work and escape into substance abuse or other retreats from the world (Krugman, 1995).

Recent research on the expectations and limitations that gender roles put on girls shows that boys have been left behind (Rich, 2018). The socialization to masculinity can be equated to such things as domination, aggression, emotional control, and reliance on self to the rise in mental health issues among men and boys, including increases in depression, violence, suicidal ideation and suicide, and overall low quality of health and well-being (Rich,

2018). These gender stereotypes essentially have not changed in the past thirty years and this fact continues to put our boys at risk in many ways (Haines, Deaux, and Lofaro, 2016).

Parents prize their boys and want them to be whole, healthy individuals who are capable of caring for others, contributing to society, finding a life path that gives them a sense of purpose and passion, and eventually raising their own children; yet, there are few guideposts and mentors to help them along the way (Haines et al., 2016). It is important to find encouraging and concrete models for helping boys and young men succeed.

WHAT PARENTS VALUE IN THEIR SONS

Chu (2014) includes as part of her research on boys' socialization to masculinity questions with parents about what they value and wish to preserve in their boys. These characteristics are those that they hope to nurture, but they are not always certain how to do so. Chu (2014) spoke with both mothers and fathers on this topic, and her findings are poignant.

Fathers were most apt to speak of boys' spunk, openness, and attunement. In the term "spunk," fathers saw the high energy, vibrancy, and exuberance of their sons; yet, they differentiated these terms from rowdiness or rambunctiousness that is so often ascribed to boys (Chu, 2014). Fathers also saw that spunk could be perceived as joyfulness and friendly and "the boys' ability to be out there" (Chu, 2014, p. 167). In this quality, there was a willingness for the boy to express himself openly, feel relatively comfortable in his own skin, and trust others to support him. The fathers, however, recognized that such openness could lead to criticism and even rejection or mockery, as these were not typical macho behaviors (Chu, 2014). This was a delicate balance for parents and sons.

Fathers also admired and hoped to nurture their sons' eagerness to explore, to dive fully into experiences, to fail, and to be uninhibited. They liked how boys got "fired up" (Chu, 2014, p. 171) about things but again realized that living full throttle was not consonant with expectations in many venues—especially schools. Boys' attitude of not necessarily caring about social expectations could be freeing to them as individuals but boded poorly for their performance in structured situations in which appropriate behavior was expected.

Chu (2014) relates that fathers also delighted in the ways in which their sons approached boy-to-boy friendships. Dads commented on the closeness and the delight in having playmates and friends, as well as the fact that such closeness enabled boys to withstand volatility in relationships without the necessity of terminating them abruptly (Chu, 2014). Boys, the dads saw, could be best friends playing, then angry at each other, and then rough housing again the next day without much need to negotiate or process.

Chu (2014) also asked fathers what they worried about most with their sons. Because they were reminiscing about their own boyhoods, the men worried about their sons coming under the social impress that dictates "the cultural norms of masculinity and societal expectations for boys and men" (Chu, 2014, p. 173). Looking ahead, the fathers saw a difficult passage into the world of proscribed male roles and remembered their own feelings of loneliness, vulnerability, and loss. Learning to adapt behavior from private to public settings forced boys away from some of their relational presence and spontaneity.

Fathers saw at an early age that their sons were experiencing gendered norms in which if they appeared to be too soft, too caring, too emotional, they became targets because they were vulnerable (Chu, 2014). Boys also had to "bluff," (Chu, 2014, p. 175) as one father put it, in order to get through situations in which they could not live up to those norms. Another said that it was not safe for boys to be "too exposed [because it makes it likely that they would be] slapped down" (Chu, 2014, p. 175).

Becoming more guarded or shielded in their emotions, boys learned to put up a tough guy front and to detach. When faced with separations or transitions, boys were pushed to be more independent and express fewer emotions of sadness, yet fathers admitted that they wanted to stay close and wanted to be able to express their sadness when separations were necessary (Chu, 2014). When fathers were asked what was wrong with displaying this emotion during separations, however, they related the pressure they felt to help their sons learn what could be expressed in private and in public so that they would not be ridiculed and rejected for openly sharing such feelings (Chu, 2014).

The fathers were willing to plumb their own experiences to find healthier options for parenting than they felt had been available to them; they also wanted boys to have a wide range of close relationships so that they had a network of people to whom they might turn in emotional dilemmas or emergencies (Chu, 2014). The fathers were aware that boys needed to be given language to express their emotions and they wanted their sons to experience a wide range of emotions and also to see their fathers' mistakes in the light of "positive models for screwing things up and it being O.K." (Chu, 2014, p. 185).

Chu's (2014) mothers described their experiences by talking about the challenges inherent in trying to truly understand their sons. Even with these challenges, they valued boys' loyalty and protectiveness as well as appreciated that their sons seemed very attuned to what was going on with them (Chu, 2014). The mothers found themselves able to be more in the moment with their sons than with daughters and enjoyed how their boys could ignore external perceptions and values on their behavior and expressions (Chu, 2014). This gave the mothers a space to act in the same way when interacting with them.

They shared the fathers' concerns about social impressions and the influence of intense social tribes and their rules (Chu, 2014). These hierarchies of peer group culture had weight in neighborhoods, schools, and other social spaces. Mothers had observed anxiety and confusion in their sons as they tried to figure out where they fit in and with whom they could feel comfortable (Chu, 2014). Not knowing or not being comfortable with going along with the rules of these cultures left boys in precarious positions; sometimes, they were socially ostracized but other times they were mocked, taunted, or even physically bullied. Chu (2014) shared a quote by one mother who said, "it makes you realize how much work it is for them just to do what looks to adults like fun" (p. 194).

Mothers could clearly see that their sons still wanted to stay close to them and receive their comfort and support, but they recognized that simultaneously, becoming a big boy did not allow for this (Chu, 2014). How to stay closely connected without impeding their sons' entry into greater independence and boyhood was mysterious to them. One mother conjured up the image of her son standing with a stuffed rabbit in one hand and a toy gun in the other as a perfect visual representation of the dilemma of wanting to maintain physical and emotional close proximity while encouraging more autonomous steps (Chu, 2014). The mothers echoed the fathers' desire to help their sons hang on to their joie de vivre, lively temperaments, openness of expression, and fierce loyalties, while at the same time being successful at navigating boy culture (Chu, 2014).

RECOGNIZE THE POWER OF THE BOY CODE

Pollack (1998, 2001) deepens the national conversation about boys' well-being by discussing the potential damage that the boy code can have. A set of expectations and behavioral rules, the boy code weans boys from their feminine side and tutors them to keep their emotions under wraps and under control. Pollack (1998) argues that the boy code impedes males' potential to connect with others and themselves by forcing separation and independence, often long before a boy is ready to handle it; thus, when young boys still need emotional nurturing and deep connection, they are urged into a "pseudo-independence" by other boys, social rituals, and even their parents (Pollack, 1998).

The boy code teaches young males to suppress emotions, but if they cannot do so, they are shamed (Pollack, 1998). By the time they enter elementary school, they are aware that if they express too much emotion, fight against separation, or reject elements of the code, such as being the "sturdy oak or big wheel" or exhibiting behavior that is deemed sissy or even rebelling against the concept that "boys will be boys" they can be taunted, bullied, ignored, or left out (Pollack, 1998).

Parents must first understand the boy code and its impress in order to be able to aid their sons, in this way they can then take active steps to break the code (Pollack, 1998). Rather than expecting boys to tough it out or problem solve beyond their developmental capacities, parents need to give their sons undivided attention on a daily basis. This occurs in the form of empathic listening, being present, and showing yourself to be a constant source of support if and when he needs it.

Breaking the boy code, Pollack (2001) argues, is not impossible, but it is dependent upon encouraging boys' "real" voices to emerge and be heard. This happens when parents give their sons undivided attention every day, even if the sons aren't ready to discuss or share at the moment (Pollack, 1998). Encouraging boys not to be afraid to express a full range of human emotions and validating those emotions when they are shared teaches boys that others will be receptive to their fear, pain, hurt, and sadness. Pollack (2001) urges parents to begin using emotionally expressive language, asking questions, and tuning in to nonverbal cues as soon as their sons are born. Since boys are not as developed in the language domain, modeling early and often the way people express emotions can boost their ability to do so (Berk, 2017).

Pollack (1998) also stresses that there is no such thing as too much love or empathy with sons. Despite social pressures to cut boys loose earlier than girls, forcing boys to stand on their own or tough out emotional difficulties in order to help them become men, boys do not turn into sissies or become feminized by keeping close ties (Berk, 2017). Instead, knowing each boy as an individual and recognizing when milestones and transitions are developmentally appropriate for him leads to confident young males who know that they have their parents in their corner when they need them (Pollack, 2001).

While there are things that parents can and should do, there also are things they should avoid such as using shaming language and techniques, as shame is a powerful deterrent to boys' willingness to open up. It has been observed that whether or not they intend to do so, parents are more apt to shame boys than girls. Pollack (1998) suggests asking open-ended questions when confused, disappointed, or disturbed by their sons' behaviors, trying to get to the heart of what the true motivations and emotions behind a behavior may be.

Pollack (1998) also exhorts parents, particularly men, not to tease or taunt their sons, even though put-downs and sarcasm are at the root of much healthy male bantering and bonding. Again, asking open-ended questions aimed at uncovering how an experience felt to the boy is a more powerful approach.

Anger and sullenness are perhaps two of the expressions most frequently associated with boys. Behaviorally, they are expected to act out. Pollack (1998) dismisses a high degree of aggression, frequent rambunctiousness, or angry actions as normal behavior and instead views them as indirect requests for help or attention. Finding a comfortable setting in which sons might be more apt to open up, parents can then try to plumb the depths of what feelings are motivating their behavior. With young boys or those who are not particularly fluent in the language of emotions, acting out may be seen as a harboring of feelings of sadness, hurt, or other kinds of emotional upset (Pollack, 1998).

Boys learn that the primary message that comes from this type of intervention is that it is not necessary to always be "the sturdy oak." Boys, Pollack (2001) explains, see models of men who are always tough, always strong, always the one other people can lean on; they come to believe that they must be emotionally hard, able to stand up to life's slings and arrows. What boys really need are grown men who share their own fears and vulnerabilities, who are honest about their feelings, so that boys can be mentored into the same kind of genuine emotional exchange (Pollack, 2001).

This advice is part of a broader strategy to present boys with models of masculinity that defy narrow stereotypes and are broad and inclusive (Pollack, 2001). This sort of parenting encourages boys in all of their passions, their chosen activities, and the relationships that they choose to develop. It is also comfortable in showing boys that those who defy gender stereotypes in the pursuit of what they care deeply about are just as much men as those who choose more traditional paths (Jean and Buckley, 2019). While some parents may be uncomfortable with those who are "gender benders," they need to assure their sons that there are myriad forms of true masculinity.

HOW TO RAISE EMOTIONALLY HEALTHY BOYS

Reist (2015) articulates some foundational practices for raising healthy boys. First, it is necessary to define the term "emotionally healthy," which entails noting that those who are emotionally healthy do not block their feelings but let them flow, as emotions are connected to what we think (Reist, 2015). Reist (2015) likens emotions to the flowing stream where water naturally flows, but if it is dammed, the water (emotions) floods the surrounding land. When the river overflows its banks, it causes damage and destruction.

> When I talk about raising emotionally healthy boys, I am not talking about what we need to do to them. I am talking about what we must avoid doing. Children are born with powerful, healthy, fully functioning emotional lives. Why then does the happy, spontaneous child develop into an angry, depressed teenager? Sometimes the answer lies in chemistry, but more often the answer

lies in the environment in which he finds himself. This environment includes all the people who clip, trim, water, and fertilize this young plant. (Reist, 2015, p. 12)

Parenting can either be an opportunity for replicating old patterns of behavior, usually inherited from our own parenting, or trying something new (Reist, 2015). To do the latter, we need emotionally healthy parents, not super parents; rather, those who are good enough and open to learning from their sons, not afraid of changing and growing themselves, and willing to challenge and transcend restrictive gender roles they confront in society (Reist, 2015). They need to be continuously asking the question, "What kind of men do we want our boys to be?" Parents need to be strong, confident, and whole.

Reist (2015) defines a whole boy or man as one who is

allowed and allows himself the whole spectrum of emotional life. He is open to the emotions of others. He thinks of emotions in a positive way. He knows that they animate people and make them loveable. He is open to the light end of the emotional spectrum as well as the dark end. He can laugh and cry. He can feel joy as well as anger. He is capable of intimacy—with women, children, and other men. (p. 17)

This is a critically important definition, as in many ways, it flies in the face of what is seen as traditional masculinity in so many aspects of American culture.

Reist believes that our men and boys are as damaged by patriarchy as are women because they are divorced from their own emotions from an early age. Part of the reason for this divorce also lies in the fact that too many parents have been damaged by the way in which they were raised. They suffer from what he calls "narcissistic" wounds that cause them to spend their adult lives looking for the unconditional love they did not receive in their own childhoods. Being forced to do so depletes the healthy energy that they can expend on their children's well-being. Rather than being fully present to their children's needs, they unconsciously repeat unhealthy patterns they have inherited. This leaves their children forced to reparent themselves.

Unhealthy mothers and fathers, Reist (2015) writes, often parent as though they are watching a rerun of their own lives. They are constantly looking for approval from others, which makes them prone to living their lives through their children's. These unhealthy parents are afraid to be themselves or encourage their children to be who they are out of fear of being judged harshly (Reist, 2015). They have difficulty sustaining the kinds of relationships needed to prevent isolation and/or loneliness. Parents also may suffer from the need for power and control if they grew up in harshly authoritarian households (Reist, 2015). If the adults were taught to be conformists, it may be difficult to raise a boy in the way that they think is right if it deviates from social norms.

Reist (2015) urges parents of boys to see parenting through the lens of both nature and nurture. There is a need to work in concert with boys' biology and chemistry and understanding these better can help parents re-frame some of boys' behaviors in a more positive way. A prime example lies in the need to listen, be attuned to nonverbal language, and understand language differences between males and females (Reist, 2015). This is supported by brain research that shows important gender differences that have profound implications for the way we deal with our sons (Price, 2017).

Gurian (1997) and Price (2017) confirm these important differences. When males and females are put in the position of doing a spatial task, most of a boy's right hemisphere fires as male brains are strongly spatial; however, male brains are not set up to be verbal like females' brains are (Gurian, 1997; Price, 2017). Brain research shows that girls' brains are at work in more sections almost all the time; Gurian (1997) likens boys' brains to a machine that turns on to do a task and then turns off, whereas girls are activated constantly. Girls, it seems, are wired to multitask, whereas boys react to having their task-oriented thinking interrupted in negative fashion.

Girls and boys are markedly different in language acquisition and use (Northwestern University, 2008). The last thing to develop in young boys is their language abilities, which is devastating in most school settings, since they are expected to perform in the same language-driven activities as girls in kindergarten through second grade (Northwestern University, 2008). Since boys lag behind in verbal skills, they also are less proficient in reading in the early elementary years. Without as much access to emotive language, boys face difficulties in the socioemotional realms of communication. This has profound implications for parents (Gurian, 1997).

When a perceived behavioral infraction is discussed with boys, both language speed and the production of the flow of words should be slowed down. This is especially important for mothers and female teachers to remember as research has shown that women tend to produce language much more quickly and easily than most males as well as processing it emotionally at a faster pace (Northwestern University, 2008). Listening, being comfortable with periods of silence, and even walking away from a conversation and returning to it at a later date are strategies necessary for processing with boys.

Reist (2015) also mentions that in adolescence, testosterone levels rise dramatically, and testosterone is known to inhibit language production in the brain. When parents, teachers, or others argue with boys, a disadvantage occurs and young men feel powerless to engage in effective verbal argument and emotional processing (Northwestern University, 2008). This explains why they frequently shut down, leave, or become aggressive. Giving them the chance to walk away without that action being seen as disrespectful and allowing them time to more slowly process their feelings and come up with their responses permits them both to maintain their dignity and to produce the answers that they really wish to share. Stressed-out or anxious adults, or those who see their own authority being challenged, are rarely able to accomplish this task (Reist, 2015).

Boys communicate just as much as girls do, but in very different ways. Reist (2015) reminds us that,

> The female brain generally prefers words. The male brain is typically more comfortable with actions as a mode of communication and therefore more comfortable with silence. Mothers need to trust that deep communication can occur when there is no talking. Women sometimes wish that their husbands (or their teenage sons) would be more verbal. . . . Men and boys often communicate more easily through their actions. Doing something for someone can be a male's way of saying "I love you." Of course, words have their value, but we need to reclaim the value of actions, of non-verbal communication, which may say even more than words could. (p. 40)

Boys' brains and male hormones will predispose boys to process feelings and emotions in male modes (Gurian, 1997). This is particularly true during the ages of five to ten, when many parents recognize changes in the way their sons process emotions and take care of their needs (Berk, 2017). The kinds of "boy-specific" ways in which they do this can help parents better respond to their sons. Gurian (1997) categorizes eight internal processing methods; however, the most employed by boys and adolescent males include:

- Action-release: processing and releasing feelings through some sort of angry action such as yelling or slamming a door.
- Suppression-delayed reaction: delaying any response, sometimes for what seems like a very long time to parents. This is because the male brain is a problem-solving brain and it may take time for a boy to identify what is troubling him and then find the words to express it.
- Displacement-objectification method: emotions are projected onto objects or turned into a story or myth so that they become less intimate and more able to be expressed.
- Physical expression: providing a "safe" space, such as a basement with a punching bag or an exercise machine where emotions can be expelled before boys return to environments in which it would not be appropriate to engage this method.
- Go into the cave: meaning that because they are slower than girls to process their emotions, they may need to retreat to their room, nature, a fort, or some other refuge to take time out. Boys, it is noted, can take up to seven hours longer than girls to process emotional data.

Gurian (1997) mentions that, while it is important to allow boys this liberty, it is necessary to hold them accountable for sharing their thoughts and insights upon their return.

Parents must carefully choose the moments for talking about feelings, since it is already clear that this is not the natural method for boys, especially under time pressure. It is a delicate balance between asking enough times to show that the parent cares about the child's feelings and not becoming overwhelmingly pestering so that he shuts down. Since boys' brains already are wired to task-orientation and problem solving, this is another method that may yield better results since solving problems releases the "emotive energy" of the experience. Gurian (1997) also mentions that if vulnerable, boys may also cry and should not be chastised for doing so, especially under very stressful conditions.

Within the last decade, practitioners are touting the benefits of such methods as meditation and mindfulness (Kabat-Zinn, 2005; Ortner, 2013). Some school systems have adopted alternative approaches to discipline aimed at teaching all students self-regulation skills and decreasing academic time lost to discipline and punishments (Mindful Schools, 2019). Yoga, meditation, and mindfulness have replaced other methods, and while critics initially scoffed at these programs, recent empirical data are showing support for these programs being integrated into our schools (Mindful Schools, 2019).

Robert W. Coleman Elementary School in West Baltimore was featured in a CNN story on its novel disciplinary program following a highly upset student as he was sent to the meditation room after name-calling with another student devolved into physical aggression (Bloom, 2016). As the student recalls, doing deep breathing, eating a snack, and pulling himself together in a quiet spot allowed him to regain composure and apologize to his class. The Mindful Movement Room includes throw pillows, yoga mats, and diffused scents; students request to go there or are sent there to stretch, calm their emotions, practice yoga, meditate, or do deep breathing to balance their feelings out until they can safely return to their classrooms in a peaceful manner (Bloom, 2016).

School staff members assist in the process as they talk with students sent to the room; a primary function of these discussions is to demonstrate the use of deep breathing to de-escalate students' emotions until they can understand their infractions and propose alternative solutions (Bloom, 2016). This kind of approach is particularly valuable because the school's population is over-represented with children who reside in homeless shelters, impoverished and violent neighborhoods (Mindful Schools, 2019).

Gaining life skills that can be used to mediate conflict or defuse stressful situations is paramount to future mental health and well-being. Every student at the school starts and finishes his school days with fifteen minutes of guided meditation; they also can practice yoga during and after school.

Bloom (2016) references a study cited in the *Journal of the American Medical Association* that reports that mindful meditation helps individuals to lessen their anxiety, pain, and depression. Parents should explore whether their sons' schools have such programs and also consider such practices in their own homes.

Ebert and Flynn (2014) discuss a program called Yoga 4 Classrooms. This program was developed in conjunction with the University of Massachusetts (Lowell) and Brigham and Women's Hospital (Harvard Medical School). Follow-up studies on the stress hormone cortisol and behavior in second and third grade students show that a classroom yoga and meditation program appears to have salutary effects on the children's behavior in school (Ebert and Flynn, 2014). Those who participated in the program lowered cortisol levels and made gains in their creativity, were more likely to control their behavior, and showed greater ability to manage anger (Ebert and Flynn, 2014).

Boys and Mothers

Reist (2015) writes about the relationship between boys and their mothers as this is one of the most frequently discussed topics throughout the history of psychology. He begins by reminding the reader that men can never have the intensity of connection on the biological and emotional level because they lack the experience of giving birth (although he fails to mention that there are instances such as adoption or surrogate births that level the playing field). Conversely, Reist (2015) mentions that contemporary society and its economic demands place women at a disadvantage since as primary caregivers still in most families, they juggle more of the role conflicts between caregiving and work responsibilities.

There is still much disagreement over the mother-son bond and the separation between the two (Winston and Chicot, 2016). All boys need to make the step toward more independence, but at what time developmentally, and in what manner depends a great deal on each individual child. Generally, society labels boys who are slower to make the separation as "mama's boys" or sees them as clingy, babyish, or wimpy (Kastner, 2018; Moon, 2018). The boy code reinforces the notion that it's not a good thing to be viewed "as a baby" but instead to step out as a "real man" would (Kastner, 2018). For some boys, it is necessary to pretend to be ready to become more individuated than they emotionally are just to keep the critics at bay.

Some parents, Reist (2015) notes, are fearful of being perceived as hanging on to their sons too long and may push them toward greater separation before they are emotionally ready. The author directs parents to the pioneering work of Chess and Thomas (1996) on temperament in children to help them gauge and better understand their sons' unique personalities and how best to parent them. This may also help the parent determine the best threshold for their son's moving outside his comfort zone.

Fathers and mothers must work in collaboration in terms of helping their sons launch, as too often fathers are more comfortable with boundary-pushing and risk-taking. As Reist (2015) points out, "the downside of this scenario is that Dad can get cast in the role of the adventurous risk-taker, while Mom gets cast in the role of the cautious worrier," (p. 96) thus, further perpetuating stereotypes.

Kindlon and Thompson (2000) speak of the trajectory of the mother-son relationship as one of both connection and alteration as:

> It is common to regard a mother's connection to her son as finite, an inevitable casualty of a boy's growth into manhood. Certainly, there comes a point in his young life when a boy must shift his central attachment from his mother to his father and begin to identify himself as a man-in-the-making. However, there is no point—not at age four, or nine, or thirteen, when a boy must "give up" his mother, or when a mother must "give up" her son. (p. 116)

Wanting to preserve the closeness but not knowing how plagues mothers of growing boys and boys are beleaguered by the message that they must give up the things most tightly associated with mothers (intimacy, emotions, love, nurturing) in order to transition into men (Kindlon and Thompson, 2000).

Many mothers had difficulty adapting their familiar routines with their sons and creating new ones without feeling sadness, alienation, or threat (Kindlon and Thompson, 2000). Mothers should find ways to calibrate their expressions of closeness to their growing sons' comfort levels. This involves being able to read their sons' needs at different times, not to fear letting go of the reins, making room for the importance of new relationships, yet simultaneously being a source of encouragement, physical closeness, and emotional expression when it is sought out (Kindlon and Thompson, 2000).

Fatherhood

Reaching emotionally healthy fatherhood requires a fundamental redefinition of what it means to be male, Reist (2015) argues. Among the many attributes of "whole" fathers are that they meet their commitments to family and society, are interested in learning from their children, have a connection to nature, respect women and those who are of different backgrounds, are empathic, spend time with their children, are emotionally expressive, take care of their own health, and are comfortable in their own bodies and with a nurturing touch (Raeburn, 2014; Reist, 2015). Fathers have an indispensable role to play in helping boys bridge the transition from separating from mother and moving into the larger world, including entering the tribe of men (Erickson, 2018; Reist, 2015).

This transition cannot be accomplished smoothly and confidently if fathers are physically or emotionally absent, leaving the boy with no guide on the trail. "Male identity, like male energy, is transferred through physical proximity, action, and words. Boys need fathers, or other significant males in their lives, to spend time with them doing things. This is how boys learn to be men" (Reist, 2015, p. 101). There is a dearth of stable, mixed-age groups to which boys can belong; activities are segregated by age, kind of activity, or setting and contemporary boys rarely have the opportunity to come together (outside of the sports arena) in ongoing mixed-age groups in which the men can help them learn their roles and statuses, model positive masculinity, and initiate them into the various stages of manhood (Reist, 2015). Boys need elders, too, yet they are difficult to find in contemporary times. With the few institutions such as churches or the Boy Scouts rocked by public sexual-abuse scandals, there is also hesitancy about giving up our boys to anyone outside the tribe (Boyle, 2012).

Kindlon and Thompson (2000) discuss desire and distance, which de-marked the yearning that both have to love and be loved, to raise sons well and be raised by caring fathers who teach their boys what it is to be a whole man. The most "emotionally resourceful and resilient boys" (Kindlon and Thompson, 2000, p. 96) are those whose fathers are there for them, who care and demonstrate it in myriad ways, and who are consistent in their support of their sons. Our culture, however, makes this kind of fathering extremely difficult given the traditional division of fiscal labor and relationship labor and the schism between men's work and women's work.

Even caring fathers are often forced to be too frequently absent from their sons' early childhoods due to the exigencies of career pursuit (Kindlon and Thompson, 2000). Most men also are not trained to care for infants and many parent in active ways that are deemed less appropriate for the young. By the time they have reached a level of career security or at least financial stability, they have been long absent. In middle childhood, when Erikson (1980) sees boys as "purposeful," sons need fathers who can help them develop and celebrate their growing competence in many arenas. How this is accom-plished has a great deal to do with the inner confidence and competence the father feels himself, especially in the emotional domain. Asking boys ques-tions and modeling behaviors that imply that it is fine not to be the "sturdy oak" all of the time can accomplish this goal of developing boys who feel comfortable in their own skins (Pollack, 1998).

Adolescence is a difficult time for both fathers and sons because of the social pressure on boys to seem invulnerable; while sons still need their fathers for emotional support, the latter may be loath to give it (Kindlon and Thompson, 2000). Tensions between boys and their peer groups and fathers further complicate the relationship. Most teenagers feel less well-known by their fathers during adolescence than during previous childhood stages

(Kindlon and Thompson, 2000). These young men took the greatest pleasure in their relationships with their fathers when the activities were mutual and reciprocal—that is, the son could teach things to the father and he was open to learning as well as leading.

According to Kindlon and Thompson (2000), too many fathers parenting adolescents fell into the trap of competing with their sons and tended to control activities rather than take part in the aforementioned reciprocal kinds of experiences. The authors describe fathers as the people most infrequently sought out to discuss emotional issues and the most likely disciplinarians in the household.

In order to close the emotional gap, fathers are encouraged not to worry if their relationship with their sons looks nothing like that with their mothers (Kindlon and Thompson, 2000). Taking part in activities together, even ones that involve little discussion, are the ways in which most dads express affection, whether these involve tossing a ball, doing a project, camping, fishing, or going out for a Sunday breakfast. Taking on some of the more traditional mother activities, such as tucking a boy in, reading a bedtime story, or taking a boy shopping can fit the bill as long as there is "a legacy of love" (Kindlon and Thompson, 2000, p. 114).

Above all else, fathers matter significantly (Raeburn, 2014). The "father hunger" that so many men in Osherson's (1986) studies express can do lasting damage developmentally, yet the presence of consistent fathers and father figures, even if they are not blood relatives, has the power to quell that hunger and provide a living, breathing model of positive masculinity.

HOW TO RAISE A HEALTHY BOY

Woolston (2017) shares several strategies for raising healthy, well-rounded sons beginning with the familiar caution to let boys show their emotions rather than expecting them to "buck up," hold back tears, or suppress anger. The author warns that boys tend to be stifled, while girls have a freer rein to express what they are feeling. Unless a boy is being destructive or cannot control himself, he should be allowed to be expressive; once he has done so, he is more likely to be able to regain control, which provides parents with an opportunity to get to the bottom of what he is really experiencing (Woolston, 2017). Parents then can help him talk about what he is feeling and why he thinks he is feeling this way. Adults may need to assist a boy in labeling or applying language to those feelings, which often means getting beyond surface anger to emotions of sadness, fear, abandonment, or hurt.

Gruber and Borelli (2017) discuss the importance of fostering emotional diversity in boys because they are raised in an environment that is inhabited by a more restricted range of emotions. The authors cite research that shows that, despite our societal tendencies to only want to experience positive emotions, humans are better off experiencing "emodiversity" (Gruber and Borelli, 2017, n.p.) just as natural environments benefit from biodiversity! Humans who experience emodiversity are more attuned to their environment, since emotions help individuals pay attention to important markers in the environment, such as warnings or other information we need to process. Those who are attuned and who experience a wider range of emotions have a greater emotional well-being as well as fewer symptoms of depression, less anxiety, fewer hospital visits, and less inflammation (Gruber and Borelli, 2017).

Gruber and Borelli (2017) argue for parents to nurture this emotional diversity in early childhood and note that it is particularly important that we do so with young boys because even in infancy, boys and girls have different emotional landscapes. Parental responses to language used with the different sexes emerge right after birth. Parents use a more emotional vocabulary with their daughters while their emotional vocabulary with their sons tends to be more primarily focused on anger. Whether this is conscious or not, parents raise their young sons in a world that is "inhabited by a narrower range of emotions" (Gruber and Borelli, 2017, n.p.).

Parents and others pay attention to their expressions of anger or acting out; yet, they are less likely to cultivate fragile emotions and the language to describe those emotions. The authors find this last fact even more disturbing due to research from Harvard Medical School (Weinberg, Tronick, Cohn, and Olson, 1999) that demonstrates that in infancy and early childhood, boys are actually the more emotionally expressive gender; however, something happens in the following years that impacts this ability; the most likely culprit is parental and societal messages about what are appropriate emotional displays for each gender.

Gruber and Borelli (2017) stress the importance of emotional diversity and expression by pointing to evidence that children who are in denial of their own emotional vulnerability are at greater risk for later unhealthy behaviors, such as substance abuse. As males traverse the life span, they more frequently suppress feelings of fragility, leading them to greater risk of depression and more acts of physical violence and anger as emotional releases (Gruber and Borelli, 2017).

In their home lives, men share less with their domestic partners and hence are less interested when their partners attempt to share with them. Emotional suppression can lead to physiological problems as well as increased risk for stress-related health problems such as heart attacks (Schneiderman, Ironson, and Seigel, 2005). Parenting young boys and adolescents to experience and express a wide range of emotions—including those that they fear make them less of a man—actually lead to healthier development over the life course (Gruber and Borelli, 2017).

It is vital that parents are physically expressive with their sons, since research has shown that parents tend to have less physical contact with their sons than with their daughters (Gruber and Borelli, 2017). What contact they do have tends to be roughhousing play or disciplinary, rather than the hugs and cuddles they bestow on their daughters; yet all children need physical closeness and comfort to help them develop a sense of security. It may be harder to do this as boys grow older, especially if they are in the presence of their peers. Physical contact may need to be more subtle or private with boys.

Keltner (2018) and Hattori (2014) both write of the importance of touch in cultivating compassion and connection in boys and men. Keltner (2018) calls touch "the primary means for spreading compassion" (n.p.); in his research, pairs of strangers participating in the study were separated by a barrier in the lab and were asked to guess the emotions the stranger was trying to convey through a one-second touch to their forearm. With only an 8 percent chance of guessing correctly randomly, participants were able to guess compassion more than 60 percent of the time and other emotions such as gratitude, anger, fear, and love more than 50 percent of the time (Keltner, 2018). Interestingly, when a man tried to communicate compassion to a female stranger, she had no idea what he was conveying and when women tried to convey anger to men, they never guessed correctly (Keltner, 2018).

Touch, Keltner (2018) notes, can help premature babies thrive and gain weight and can turn off the "threat switch" in the brain if a romantic partner is undergoing stress. Participants in a game in which they could choose to cooperate or compete with a partner were far more likely to share and be cooperative, even for a monetary prize, if gently touched by the experimenter (Keltner, 2018). Touch, therefore, has been proposed as therapy and as an expression of love that parents can share with their children, and this is equally important for sons as it is for daughters.

Boys at Play

All children, naturally, begin as highly sensory beings who need to be exposed to all the senses and have rich sensory lives (Berk, 2017). They also begin as energetic beings, boys particularly so. Boys are aware of their own energetic nature and seek to find ways to express those energies within the confines of acceptable behavior; however, this is often difficult to do. Reist (2015) acknowledges that boys need both freedom and structure—or actually "freedom within structure" (p. 53) and urge readers to consider how boys would be able to find this within healthy athletic experiences.

These athletic experiences, when coached correctly, provide a perfect example of good discipline in everyday life because they have clear goals, well-articulated and understood rules, and enforce fairness for all (Reist, 2015). Boys accept this structure because the inherent rules and structures have reasonable purposes, can be comprehended, and are easy to obey; further, in good coaching and good disciplining, the end goal is teamwork, respecting the worth of each individual, stressing his contribution to the ultimate goal, and using praise and motivation to improve performance (Reist, 2015).

Boys have a great deal of energy that can get them and others around them frustrated if they do not have adequate opportunities to expend pent-up energy through activities that allow them to run, climb, manipulate objects, explore, and just generally blow off steam (Bento and Dias, 2017). While boys need to learn the limitations of physical play in certain circumstances, they also benefit from environments that are created with some of their needs in mind (Bento and Dias, 2017). Child care settings, schools, and other locales that are meant to invite them, such as creative libraries and children's museums, recognize that they will not be able to hold in their natural tendencies for long periods of time.

The best settings for boys, whether they are home or away, include lots of objects that can be manipulated; plenty of space; little screen time; caregivers who understand and enjoy boy energy; and environments that encourage boys to take healthy risks (Gurian, 1997). Woolston (2017) adds that the best settings for raising healthy boys also have a wide variety of options in terms of activities and don't worry if boys pick stations or activities that aren't seen as "masculine." Playing in a kitchen, cuddling a stuffed animal, interacting with dolls, or other activities should be encouraged, as they help boys develop skills that are extremely useful in adulthood.

Reist (2015) echoes this theme, writing that,

> As girls grow up, they are permitted, indeed even encouraged, to pursue a wide range of activities, even those considered traditionally male. Boys have not had the same kind of liberation. They avoid any activities or behaviours that are seen as feminine. These are gay. Whole areas of human life become out of bounds or require great personal courage to enter. (p. 129)

When respected adults and older peers engage in these activities or encourage them, boys have a wide spectrum of resources from which to pick activities that have goodness of fit for their personalities and interests.

Most boys also need activities that help them form close, intimate relationships and hone their social skills since they have been found not to form intimate friendships as easily as girls (Olsen, 2017). Their play tends to be structured into groups with hierarchies of leadership that require boys to constantly negotiate for a higher spot. Cooperative play and one-on-one play-dates help with balancing these more natural tendencies (Olsen, 2017).

Parents should encourage their sons' interests, whether they are labeled "boy" activities or not (Woolston, 2017). A boy who wants to take ballet, for example, may be teased by his friends (and even some adults), but supporting these choices early in life helps build an internal compass and the strength to accept differences in other people, as well as in oneself.

Reist (2015) tackles the controversy surrounding boys and aggressive play, especially with toy guns. Without taking sides regarding war play and guns, these are necessary elements of boys' play, the most traditional use of these activities is to be "assertive, competitive, goal-oriented" (Reist, 2015, p. 132) and protective, in that boys fight together to defeat monsters, common enemies, or those that threaten their territory. In the majority of cases such actions have nothing to do with pathology, and if boys are denied the props of such play, they find other weapons in the natural world to substitute (Reist, 2015).

Reist (2015) and others address the growing number of hours and amount of energy that screen time and video games are taking up among boys and offer that these have much to teach about parenting. The foundational principles identified out of involvement with video games include the need to move in space; the need for power and control; the need to have concrete goals; the need for play; and the need for territory; the need for rewards (Reist, 2015). Also highlighted is the need for dealing with emotions, for having guidance with gender roles and relationships, the need for a social life, and the addictive nature of video games for boys because they raise the level of production of dopamine in the male brain's pleasure and reward centers (Reist, 2015).

The author reframes each of these needs into other activities that boys can engage in with their parents. Each of these pressing needs can be met in a variety of ways, such as participating in activities that encourage movement through real space and stimulate the production of endorphins (such as team or individual sports or exercise), through training in emotional diversity, or through allowing greater autonomy and control over choices in their activities (Reist, 2015).

Promoting Self-Discipline

Given the exuberant nature of most young boys, it is critical for parents to help them develop the internal controls to curb their nature at appropriate times, such as at school or other arenas. Without tamping down their true selves in the interest of societal conformity, they need to internalize some behavioral guidelines while some social institutions (like elementary schools, for example), may need to make changes to better accommodate their male students.

Kindlon and Thompson (2000) write that harsh physical and verbal punishments have historically been used to help make a man out of a boy. This presumes both that boys don't respond well to subtler forms of correction and that girls should be treated differently when it comes to discipline. Both parents and teachers tend to discipline boys more frequently and harshly than girls; yet harsh discipline leads boys to shame, anger, self-loathing, and shutting down emotionally (Kindlon and Thompson, 2000). Angry, depressed boys grow up to be the same as men and their response to these forms of discipline lean toward anger, confrontation, or escape rather than compliance (Kindlon and Thompson, 2000).

Boy activity—much of it predisposed and normal—triggers many incidents of discipline; yet the primary goal of discipline is to help children internalize responsible behavioral codes. Healthy discipline is founded upon ten basic principles that include consistency in reinforcement and punishment; leadership by modeling or teaching; respect for the disciplinarian and for self; a larger spiritual context by identifying the inherent dignity of each person; and having choices. Gurian (2001) also promotes respect for other people's feelings; starting early and adapting discipline across life stages; and having an authoritative (rather than permissive or authoritarian) structure by creating "a sense of wise authority in ourselves so that the boy believes we are the right leader to listen to" (p. 168).

The foundation of self-discipline and a moral compass, which are important components of overall health and well-being, must be laid in very early childhood (Elium and Elium, 2004). In an interesting comment, the authors warn that while quality time between parents and sons is important, everyday presence and guidance is incredibly valuable. This is especially true for men in that "the father who waits to become alive in the family until his son is a teenager and making trouble puts himself at a great disadvantage. . . . Equal amounts of quality and quantity time spent with sons when they are young, especially with their fathers, is an investment that pays royally when the testosterone hits at puberty" (Elium and Elium, 2004, p. 135).

Discipline is not a democratic process; yet it must be related to the offense, be age-appropriate, realistic with rewards, and gradually negotiated as boys mature and demonstrate responsibility (Elium and Elium, 2004). To help young men grow in self-discipline and social conscience, they need to be given opportunities to express their natural gifts, speak to their mature selves, listen for positive intent in behaviors while not ignoring immature actions or words, and model ethical and moral values on a regular basis.

Elium and Elium (2004) remind the reader that boys are not the equivalent of their bad behaviors or poor choices. Slowing down to listen to the intent behind behaviors that annoy or frighten adults is one of the hardest aspects of child rearing, and it is important to catch boys being good in order to counter the more difficult moments (Dobson, 2001). Woolston (2017) mentions noticing and commenting to let them know that efforts to maintain or regain self-control and channeling inappropriate energies into activities that are appropriate are much appreciated.

Many also speak to the power of story and myth in helping boys learn character. Gurian (2000) shares that stories are the most ancient and effective tools for teaching children morals and values. He advocates using "primal" tales—ones that are relatable to contemporary life but also carry deep-grounded wisdom about how one should act. Gurian (2000) relies on archetypes such as the king, the warrior, or the explorer to stress his points and laments that current American culture is almost devoid of such stories, so that children turn to stereotypes instead.

Gurian (2000) asserts that boys are particularly in need of such stories because as they age, they feel "less and less emotionally astute and mature compared to the girls around them. Their nature and their socialization tend to lead them away from emotional literacy, while both nature and socialization tend to lead girls towards it" (p. 207). In characters and stories, they begin to develop a greater internal language to express their feelings.

By being able to relate to a person in a story, boys are aided in being able to express their emotions. This approach is challenging, however, because at the very point at which boys most need this emotional literacy, it becomes uncool to read (girl activity) so other forms of quality media may be used to augment reading and books must be carefully chosen and shared with boys.

Gurian (2000) also urges parents to bring members of the tribe into conversation about goals they have and immediate obstacles they are facing in moral and spiritual development of their sons. Thus, there are more individuals the boy treasures "on the same page" and more eyes and ears on behavioral expressions. There is a necessity in helping boys become grounded in a spiritual life (not synonymous with formal religion) by helping them ponder the big questions about what their purpose on earth is, what they believe in, what is worth living for, and how they can turn their creative powers to work for good (Gurian, 2001). Again, a vast array of connected others who love the boy can help extend the conversation on the spirit life, sharing their own experiences and bringing diverse perspectives.

Cultivating Compassion in Boys

Hattori (2014), the father of two boys himself, conducted interviews with researchers and spiritual leaders to determine how best to cultivate compassion in young boys and adolescents. His interest evolved from the wave of violence unleashed in schools and cyberspace as well as the increase in suicides nationally.

One area that he uncovered has to do with the power of touch and the emotional conveyances that touch provides. Hattori (2014) notes the awkwardness of touch around the age of eight or nine, but especially in adolescence, and quotes Kindlon and Thompson (2000) as saying "boys need to experience that physical tenderness if they are to speak the language later.

Otherwise, we leave their touch training to football coaches, wrestling opponents, and casual sex partners" (p. 2).

Being told to "be a man" implies isolating oneself from their emotions and not asking for help when struggling. Hattori (2014) says of his parenting:

> Let boys cry. When my boys cry, I comfort them and try to understand why they are suffering. I'm not worried about them becoming "crybabies"; I'm more concerned about them being trapped in the "emotional funnel" that only allows them to express anger. Helping boys to step out of traditional expectations of masculinity allows them to flourish as unique individuals rather than being confined to stereotypes. This entails being confident enough to challenge gender roles and being comfortable with "letting them dress in pink, sing songs from *Frozen*, and play with dolls, but also express their softer emotions, ask for help, and hug other boys." (p. 3)

The sympathetic men that Hattori (2014) interviewed in his study almost always had similarly compassionate male role models in their lives. If fathers are not present in boys' lives, it is necessary to find other males to be role models and to rely on them to model the kinds of qualities that "real men" possess; these role models may be relatives, mentors, neighbors, grandfathers, spiritual leaders, coaches, or teachers (Hattori, 2014).

Men are amazingly resistant to being in a state of silence and stillness (Wilson et al., 2014). In this study, men would much prefer doing routine external tasks to being alone with their thoughts for any time and, incredibly, two-thirds of them preferred giving themselves electric shocks to being alone with their emotions and thoughts (Wilson et al., 2014). Hattori (2014) points out that this aversion kept boys from the new three Rs (1) relationship, (2) resilience, and (3) reflection.

Many schools are finding that boys are much less likely to have disciplinary problems when they are taught mindfulness from a very young age and when they can be sent to a meditation room to reflect on their actions rather than being disciplined in traditional ways (Bloom, 2016; Jean and Rotas, 2019; Mindful Schools, 2019). Building such practices into daily life early on, providing compassionate role models, and using reflection and mindfulness as ways of breaking cycles of acting out are all techniques that parents can incorporate (Brown and Olson, 2015). These, in addition to cultivating emotional diversity and being comfortable in challenging gender roles and stereotypes, are some of the best gifts they can give their young sons to prepare for a healthy future (Jean and Buckley, 2019).

ELEVATING THE EMOTIONAL LIVES OF BOYS

PBS Parents (n.d.) captures many of the salient strategies for understanding and raising boys and shares them on their website regularly. Online posts distill wisdom from Kindlon and Thompson's classic 2000 book, *Raising Cain: Protecting the Emotional Life of Boys.* The first of those strategies is to help boys develop an inner life by supporting their display of the entire spectrum of human emotions. By assuming that boys have an equally rich internal life, parents can help them accept and articulate their emotions. This is particularly important due to research by Weinberg et al. (1999) that shows boys begin life more vulnerable and less resilient than girls, contrary to popular myth.

Girls were more able to calm themselves; however, boys got more easily distressed and were less able to return to a state of calm (Weinberg et al., 1999). By recognizing that as infants, boys experience emotions such as fear, shame, uncertainty, and humiliation—even though boys are viewed as being tough or resilient from birth, parents can understand that their sons have vulnerabilities that need to be considered. Given this knowledge, Kindlon and Thompson (2000) suggest that boys should be raised in a different manner than is the current prescription for masculinity.

A second suggestion from Weinberg et al. (1999) stated that adults must embrace the high level of activity that boys possess. While the intent is to prevent boys from being hurt or endangering themselves or others, giving them safe spaces permits the healthy expression of boy energy in manageable ways. Too often, boy energy is seen as a threat to order in homes, classrooms, and other social settings; helping boys channel this exuberance into appropriate activities and venues honors their physicality while teaching them to gauge the level of expression that fits each setting (Weinberg et al., 1999).

Kindlon and Thompson (2000) urge parents to find ways to speak to boys in the boys' language. This entails honoring their pride and tapping into their masculine preferences to be problem solvers and consultants. Since boys are concerned about displaying too much emotion or uncovering vulnerabilities, these kinds of roles allow them to feel that they are important cogs in the problem-solving process, rather than being shamed or humiliated by being confronted (Kindlon and Thompson, 2000). While boys' answers tend to be briefer than girls', recognizing that length of response is less important than the power of connection is the key to good communication with our sons.

With contemporary media and traditional parenting teaching boys that courage is synonymous with physical courage and standing up to strong enemies, villains, or fierce beasts, a step toward raising healthy boys involves teaching them that there are other forms of courage, such as emotional courage, integrity, and advocacy for others (Goleman, 2006; Lassiter, 2017).

New definitions of courage and heroism are needed. Parents need to be intentional in pointing out acts of courage that take other shapes and forms in daily life; they must display emotional courage and personal integrity and conscience in the way they conduct themselves; and they can utilize positive forms of media (such as characters in books and movies, or athletes or celebrities who are role models in sharing their personal struggles, emotional difficulties, or acts that champion others who are less powerful) to build character (Goleman, 2006; Lassiter, 2017).

Kindlon and Thompson (2000) discuss the tricky balance in finding disciplinary strategies that work to build boys' character and conscience without making them become resistant to authority. The exuberant and physical nature of boy energy brings them into many situations that require limits or discipline. Clear, consistent, and reasonable disciplinary structures that engage boys in helping to solve behavioral problems rather than shaming, humiliating, or turning them into mortal enemies are vital (Hoyt, 2015; Kindlon and Thompson, 2000).

In healthy parenting relationships, children strive to please their parents and do not intentionally wish to disappoint them with their actions. Recognizing this, parents should avoid harsh or physical punishment, demeaning comments, and excessive anger, as these will cause boys to resist adult authority rather than shape behaviors to be more accommodating (Kindlon and Thompson, 2000). Helping boys to reframe inappropriate responses through a problem-solving mode teaches them skills that can be applied to future situations.

Slocumb (2007) suggests an alternate strategy to help parents avoid shaming boys, which essentially guarantees that their psyches will be harmed and that the goal of the shaming will not be reached voluntarily. Using the acronym HEAT, parents and educators can use a four step process to help boys process their problems (Slocumb, 2007):

- **H**ere: active listening without interruption or interjection as well as rephrasing what was heard/said ("What I hear you saying is . . . ").
- **E**mpathize: letting the boy know that you understand why he is upset and might be upset yourself if in the same situation.
- **A**pology: ("I am sorry this happened to you . . . ").
- **T**ake action: this last step is critical in helping the boy problem; it can be initiated by either offering a first step ("What I would like to offer you . . . ") or asking what the boy would like you to do in the situation.

The technique relies on respect and dignity, rather than humiliation and shame, to assist the boy in coming up with an acceptable solution to a misbehavior (Slocumb, 2007).

Boys cannot be expected to become more emotionally attached and expressive without models of how to do so. This requires that parents themselves model these characteristics and that they also seek out other males who portray the kinds of emotional openness and interactions with others that deviate from more traditional male displays of emotional distance, guardedness, fear of physical closeness, or strength through defeating others (Murray and Rosanbalm, 2017). The friendships that boys make are tricky, as they involve competitions and often verbal one-upmanship; therefore, boys need to learn from whole men how they encountered these challenges and worked through them to preserve meaningful friendships with other men that they loved and valued (Murray and Rosanbalm, 2017; Slocumb, 2007).

Like other authors, Kindlon and Thompson (2000) see good parenting as that which shows boys myriad ways to be men. The narrow definition of masculinity that is most accessible to boys confines them in so many ways; it is the job of good parents and other adults who are important to our boys' lives to praise many different avenues for boys to take, including those that may deviate from traditional gendered roles (Murray and Rosanbalm, 2017). Helping boys recognize that there are many ways to express bravery, toughness, boldness, and leadership and speaking positively about the courage of those who follow their talents and passions, even in roles that step outside the traditional norms of "masculinity," empower boys to envision a much richer concept of what it means to be men (Kindlon and Thompson, 2000).

Tartakovsky (2013) remarks on the pervasiveness of messages about masculinity in society, that many of the key figures in boys' lives are the very ones perpetuating limited stereotypes of what being a man entails to include prominent role models ranging from fathers and mothers to coaches and peers. In his work on raising emotionally healthy boys, Zeff (2013) notes that it is impossible to raise well-rounded boys if the adults themselves are emotionally repressed, reinforce unhealthy male stereotypes, and are not expressive in ways that promote compassion, openness, and qualities that support relationships.

Zeff (2013) says that emotional health necessitates one being in touch with his or her internal life and being able to express the whole gamut of emotions—even those that suggest vulnerabilities. It also entails being empathic toward others and despite what some might think, it does not equate with being a "wimp" or a "pushover" but instead requires choices to be assertive rather than aggressive. Raising healthy boys, he argues, begins with taking an honest inventory of one's own beliefs and values inherited from family and community of origin. Many unconscious attitudes and biases about what it means to be masculine may be present, and many men have been damaged by their own fathers' parenting styles.

Zeff (2013) encourages adults to read widely and to parent transparently, so that when mistakes are made, parents are not afraid to admit them. He also warns parents to monitor boys' exposure to violence, restricting cruel or violent media and games, while encouraging active, yet more positive outlets. While Zeff (2013) recognizes that as boys age and are less under their parents' watchful eye it is hard to monitor their exposure, he asserts that maintaining dialogue about what the boys are hearing and watching and how those images and words affect their emotions and thoughts is critical.

Offering role models and interventions that short-circuit aggressive or violent actions and promote cooperation are tools that promote emotional health (Zeff, 2013). This can range from service activities, team membership, faith groups, mentors, or even activities such as self-defense, karate, or tai chi, which appeal to boys for their combination of the physical and the mental. Using the aforementioned boy-as-consultant or problem-solver model when aggression does confront him gives children practice in alternative ways to resolve issues (Slocumb, 2007).

Emotional health is the result of parents and other significant figures becoming psychologically attuned to their children (Firestone, 2012). Contemporary parents, often through no fault of their own, are perilously distracted from children's emotional worlds and this work, when done, most often falls to females (Firestone, 2012). There is a general tendency in today's society to pay more attention to our children's behaviors than to their emotions.

Firestone (2012) offers parenting principles that help maintain awareness of children's feelings so that we can be aware of dangers and promote prosocial, healthy development. Among these is being aware of behavioral changes that could signal that a boy is struggling; subtle changes will not be noticed unless there is ongoing attunement. Firestone (2012) also warns not to write-off changes in moods or behaviors merely to developmental phases or stages because, while there are definitely changes in hormones and other physiological and psychological states, a parent needs to know his or her child well in order to assess whether these are typical changes or something out of the ordinary.

When parents express an interest in their concerns about their children's emotions, they help children become more self-attuned (Firestone, 2012). If children open up and honestly express the roots of their struggles, however, parents need to respond in ways that are compassionate and sensitive, not reactive or authoritarian. Helping children problem-solve ways around challenges, fears, or emotional dilemmas can bolster resiliency, as it models proactive ways of approaching one's struggles.

RECOGNIZING DIFFERENCES IN PARENTING STYLES

Elium and Elium (2004) remark on the way that a father and son relate to each other, noting that they connect deeply when they engage physically, and feeling that this is sometimes a mystery to the female parent because "their play has a different quality, as if they have their own language of grunts, farts, burps, chortles, feints, and holds. The masculine force has a ferocious-ness that demands, 'Ho! Take notice! This is real. This is important. I have a positive and creative purpose'" (Elium and Elium, 2004, p. 94).

What has been observed is borne out in research that demonstrates how differently mothers and fathers parent, for the most part. Hall (2017) cites a large study conducted in the United Kingdom that reveals that fathers were less apt to argue or fight with their children but felt deprived of conversations about their daily lives and their challenges. Fathers longed for more consis-tent relationships with their children and were not as involved with signifi-cant figures in their lives, such as teachers or other parents.

Fathers give their children more freedom and often act in more "rough and tumble" ways with sons. They are more likely to respond to their sons if they act out in anger or frustration. Vitelli (2017) points out that most studies that have looked at parenting young children have focused on mothering and that the majority of parenting studies rely on self-report, which may not be accurate. Studies that use observation and other ways of rating interactions to produce data consistently, however, show fathers engaged in physical inter-actions with sons (tickling, tumbling, poking) while using singing or whis-tling in more emotionally responsive ways with their daughters (Vitelli, 2017).

Dads also used different kinds of language with each sex, with girls receiving more emotionally tied words and boys more achievement-related words (such as proud, win, top) and their interactions appeared to reinforce greater empathy among girls and competition among boys (Vitelli, 2017). There is a question, though, of whether fathers' differential treatment of children is due to their own gender expectations or whether they react to cues in behavior that are linked to biological differences, as Vitelli (2017) notes that girls high in fetal testosterone tend to prefer more aggressive play, which may lead fathers then to respond to their preferences.

Fathers have a very different role to play in raising children, and boys learn aspects of masculinity without even being aware of it; yet men often are polarized in their parenting approaches, either wanting to be just like their fathers or anything but like their fathers (Vitelli, 2017). The role of being a father has changed dramatically during the past several generations so that the pattern of boys' development that once was derived following the father's role model, often working with or apprenticing for the father, and staying close to home in adulthood has been changed by the necessity of fathers going off to work elsewhere, with their status as men dictated less by family and community commitments and more by salary and value of their possessions (American Psychological Association, 2019).

With parenting now seen as women's work, men became more marginalized in the lives of their children and women often guarded of their domain by insisting that even fathers who wished to be actively engaged with their children should do things in a specific way (Yogman and Garfield, 2016). This can undermine fathers' confidence in relating to their children, so it is necessary that both parents see and honor the value of different styles of parenting, as mentioned earlier.

Boys who have consistently present, loving fathers have far fewer problems later in their lives in all areas (Yogman and Garfield, 2016). A longitudinal study that explores the roles of both mothers and fathers on the emotional health and empathy of boys and girls showed that the most influential factor in how emotionally healthy the children were, was dependent upon the degree of the father's involvement with them (Nilsen, Karevold, Kaasbøll, and Kjeldsen, 2018; Raeburn, 2014).

Parenting via the "Tribe"

Gurian (1997) was among the earliest to tout the value of the "tribe" in raising healthy boys; referring to it as a three family system that includes: (1) the birth or adoptive parents, (2) the extended family (including blood relatives, friends, educators, day-care providers, and mentors), and (3) culture and community groups with which the boy was involved. Consonance among and between these families is essential, so that morals, values, ethics, and messages we send about what being a real boy is are consistent and are supported in all venues.

Gurian (1997) views the four basic goals of raising emotionally healthy boys as: (1) being social and having a personal commitment to living a healthy life and giving back to society, (2) being committed to one's partner, (3) being a responsible parent of one's children, and (4) having continuous spiritual growth. A three-family shared vision as to how to accomplish these goals is necessary because the nuclear family alone is generally too taxed in hectic contemporary life to go it alone.

Gurian (1997) laments the demise of this three-family system, which was present until the end of the 1950s, when families became more mobile in search of better jobs and widened horizons. This fractured families and moved the nuclear family away from natural support systems such as relatives, neighborhood, and faith groups and other local organizations. Media and peer groups took up a larger role in "parenting" and many families began to crumble on their own.

Gurian (1997) argues that throughout history, boys and men were socialized to the tribe, which served protective and economic purposes in hunter-gatherer societies. While not suggesting the family system return to the Ozzie and Harriet model of families, or the traditional 1950s nuclear family, Gurian (1997) instead suggests looking "further back, into our ancestral past, for structural wisdom about how boy-friendly families can look, then moving forward into a future whose content—the stuff we put inside the structure—is constantly evolving. This future accepts the necessity that blood-ties and marriage vows are no longer necessarily the best definition of family" (p. 66).

The nonblood clan and family systems long embraced by Hawaiians and Mexicans and Mexican Americans, for example, offer godparents or non-blood aunts and uncles who are chosen when the child is very young (Gurian, 1997). These individuals are said "to carry the personality of the child" (p. 73). Gurian (1997) also references tribal living in which the second family, or nonblood kin, can serve as a safe haven for boys when they are in tension with their birth family. Because Americans prize individuality and independence so highly, Gurian (1997) finds that too many parents subscribe to the myth that all their sons need is them.

For the most part, American culture does not treasure and revere its elderly; thus, traditional elders are not available to impart traditions and guide boys through rites of passage (Gurian, 1997). With grandparents so frequently geographically absent, parents must look to other institutions to find elders; defined rites of passage to manhood barely exist anymore, with apprenticeships, heroic journeys, or military service absent in most boys' lives. While schools, teams, and clubs can provide mentors as boys get older, boys are more apt to seek out their own; however, their choices are easier and more appropriate when they have a rich array of positive males around them to choose from.

Parenting Boys in Nontraditional Families

Parents raising boys in nontraditional families share many of the same challenges and use many of the same strategies as those in two-parent, heterosexual households—which have been viewed as the norm until recent decades. An extraordinary number of boys grow up in homes of divorce. They must adapt to the transition from intact to newly configured family, and it is up to the parents to make this transition as healthy as possible.

Reist (2015) defines marriages and long-term, committed relationships that are not legal marriages, in terms of six separate stages: (1) honeymoon; (2) getting to know you; (3) smooth; (4) unseen cracks; (5) visible cracks; and (6) decision stage (physical separation, emotional separation, continue at stage 5, get help and redefine relationship). Where a boy's family experience falls in this process greatly influences what his reaction to a divorce is. If he experienced the smooth stage and/or stage of unseen cracks, he will have a positive view of the family and mourn its loss or reconfiguration more greatly. If he has lived through toxic periods, there may be relief. Yet above all else, how the parents deal with and explain the transition, and what the child's temperament is will have the most profound effects on the emotional outcomes (Chess and Thomas, 1996).

Boys who remain with their mothers versus boys who remain with their fathers as the primary custodians face different challenges. Those who remain with mothers generally have experienced them as the main caregiver during childhood; while this leads to a connection of mutual support and empathy, when the boy reaches adolescence and needs to move toward greater independence, he confronts a tricky situation. Some boys may feel guilty about the separation while others may overreact and abruptly push the mother away (Chess and Thomas, 1996; Reist, 2015). Those who are in their fathers' care (much less common) may experience a different type of parenting than they were provided by their mothers. In cases in which fathers are awarded custody, there usually has been a high degree of involvement in boys' lives, but as mentioned previously, there tend to be different parenting styles between men and women (Chess and Thomas, 1996; Reist, 2015).

The noncustodial parent (or if parents are joint custodians, the other parent) needs to continue to play a positive role in the boy's life, if possible, and both parents need to support each other in seeing the health of their son as more important than personal preferences or proclivities in parenting (Dobson, 2001). Divorces, separations, or other losses (such as death) can be ameliorated to some degree if a strong tribe has been built previously and if parents themselves are emotionally healthy, even during times of stress and grief. With supportive others who have been a part of the boy's life, parents have mentors and guides to lean on when their own emotional or physical resources are low. One of the most important sources of support may come in the form of grandparents or other extended family members; while contemporary society sees more and more families scattered geographically, even those who are apart can form a network to bolster boys and young men (Dobson, 2001).

Grover (2016) remarks that conducting searches about boys who are raised without their fathers is most likely to result in a negative deluge of statistics about how these fatherless boys are prone to crime, dropping out of school, substance abuse problems, incarceration, and general failure to meet their potential. Citing the research that undergirds a recent documentary called *In a Perfect World*, Grover (2016) notes the life stories of men who thrived despite being raised by single mothers alone.

He debunked three primary myths about fatherless boys. The first is that they inevitably suffer delinquent tendencies. Grover (2016) found that the label of "fatherlessness" is too simplistic, as it masks major differences in household compositions. The worst outcomes for boys are when they are raised by a mother and stepfather, and homes in which there are toxic marriages cause far greater damage to boys' emotional well-being than being raised by a single mother or a female couple.

Another myth is that being fatherless results in depression and anger issues. Instead, it was the quality of the relationships that the boys did have in their lives that influenced their well-being. The men who thrived in the documentary research were those who chose or who were gifted with positive extended family members, male mentors and role models, and other men who stepped willingly into surrogate father roles (Grover, 2016).

A final concern that has taken on mythical proportions is that if a boy does not grow up with a present father, he himself will not know how to father his children (Grover, 2016). Instead, these boys, when they became parents themselves, were highly motivated to be the fathers that they never had and were moved to share special bonds with their own children. They refused to let their own pasts define them and they demonstrated grit and resiliency that they inherited from their mothers and observed in significant adults in their lives.

Writing that men raised without their fathers present are equally likely to be successful in their lives, Grover (2016) urges adults to study history to find many examples of those in every field who did so. Men and boys raised by single mothers often are more relational and more able to read and respond to the emotions of others. The main takeaway from the documentary's research is that it is less important who may be missing from a boy's formative years than who is fully present.

Dowd (2018) and Marcoux (2018) summarize the findings of another important piece of research—that of the mental and emotional health of children who grow up in lesbian parent homes. A thirty-two-year longitudinal study (the ongoing U.S. National Longitudinal Lesbian Family Study) follows a cohort of children raised in such families. When the study first began in 1986, there was large-scale societal concern about the psychological adjustment, mental health, and emotional well-being of these children; however, findings suggest that these children fare well and that their mental and emotional health, as well as prosocial behavior, are as good as or better than those of children born to heterosexual couples (Dowd, 2018; Marcoux, 2018).

FINAL THOUGHTS

It is not easy raising sons in contemporary times. Toxic culture, the boy code, stressed and anxious parents, and economic and social pressures can interfere with developing environments and relationships that nurture boys' well-being. Many parents themselves have grown up without positive father figures in their lives, and changes in societal views about what men and women should be and how they should act has left our society with few clear roadmaps and guides to assist in helping boys grow up to be the men they should be and that our country needs them to be.

Parents and caregivers need to understand the unique characteristics and needs of boys. They are naturally wired to high energy, are slower in processing and finding words to express emotions, and need environments that respect their exuberance. Many of our institutions, such as child care centers and elementary schools, are not geared toward boys' proclivities and needs; indeed, some respond harshly to boy energy. While boys need to learn to channel their energies into appropriate behaviors in different settings, they also need to be provided with venues that tap into their inherent proclivities.

Disciplining boys is a delicate balance of providing the necessary responses to behavioral infractions while avoiding shaming boys in the process. Because they are less able than girls to process emotions quickly and find the right language to communicate those emotions, boys often withdraw, shut down, or lash out in situations in which they are expected to explain their behavioral choices. In order to keep the lines of communication open, parents may want to give boys time and space to process their thoughts and feelings. Often, the best communication occurs while boys are engaged in some sort of activity with their parents, especially their fathers or other important men.

All boys need consistent, compassionate parenting that is developmentally appropriate, attends to their emotional and spiritual life, and models the values, ethics, and morals that the family, community, and culture uphold. Parents cannot do this alone; they need to form second families or tribes, particularly in these times in which so many nuclear families are under stress and extended families may be geographically separated. Mentors, teachers, elders, and extended relatives, whether blood relatives or not, fill critical roles in raising young boys and adolescents to be good men.

Nontraditional families can be just as successful in raising emotionally healthy boys as traditional families. They rely on creating the same elements of all successful parenting relationships, such as understanding the nature of boys, recognizing the unique characteristics of each child, building networks or tribes of others to mentor and support the boys, being emotionally healthy as parents, and supporting the child as he grows into adulthood.

POINTS TO REMEMBER

- Raising boys to be emotionally healthy and "whole" is hard work in contemporary society because of the powerful impress of the boy code.

- It is difficult for parents to do this job alone; boys need tribes—mentors, elders, guides, teachers.
- Boys need support from an early age in developing emotional diversity and the language with which to express their emotions.
- Boys need to be seen as unique individuals and encouraged to follow their individual interests and talents, even if they lead them in directions that are not considered traditionally masculine.
- Boys need fathers who are physically and emotionally present and willing to parent equally, even if their parenting style is different from that of mothers.
- When disciplining boys, parents need to remember that boys need time to process their emotions and find language to describe their motivations, otherwise they will shut down, walk away, or lash out.
- Nontraditional families do just as good a job of raising their sons as do traditional families.

Chapter Five

Off the Couch and onto the Ball Court

Effective Strategies for Counseling Boys

Counselors can be essential in helping both boys and men expand their notion of masculinity and develop meaningful roles for themselves. By taking a gender-sensitive, psychoeducational stance in working with traditional male clients, counselors can broaden the very definition of masculinity. As Levant (2005) notes, "The Women's Movement succeeded in expanding women's adult roles, so that a woman can be both an aggressive marketer and a loving mother. We have yet to do the equivalent for men. We seem to fear that men will lose their essential manhood if they are not tough enough" (p. 168).

It appears from the research and professional practice of the many prominent authors of the *New Psychology of Men* (Levant and Pollack, 2005) that traditional American men find themselves in a difficult period in history—stretched thin between the demands that uphold their typical roles as breadwinners and protectors, while simultaneously being the sensitive partners, loving fathers, and egalitarian partners that are desirable post-women's movement.

Long socialized to distance themselves from the needy and vulnerable parts of themselves, and the expression of such emotions, men and boys are severely hampered when it comes to having access to and language for the relational parts of their beings. Therapy could be a powerful tool in helping them expand their roles, articulate their needs, and express their emotions; it could give rise to a generation of men who could reach their potential to be more "whole" human beings (Seidler, Rice, Ogrodniczuk, Oliffe, and Dhillon, 2018).

Unfortunately, the institution of psychotherapy has been constructed, for the most part, out of cultural dictates that are foreign to men and boys. This lack of "good fit" between what masculinity demands and what psychotherapy entails predisposes men to avoid therapy whenever possible (Seidler et al., 2018). The savvy and effective therapist—male or female— will be one who practices gender sensitive counseling and has a strong foundational knowledge of gender studies, as well as a sensitivity to traditional men and their atypical counterparts, a knowledge of themes and issues that are at the heart of their struggles, and an openness to constructing therapeutic sessions that reflect male preferences in communications and relational styles (Johnson, 2005; Scholz and Hall, 2014). As Mahalik (1999) notes,

> therapists with knowledge of male gender role conflict can help clients move toward relationships with others and integrate an emotional life into men's sense of self. That is, instead of punishing the male client for expressing his emotional needs as the media, family, and his peers have done since his earliest years, the therapist has the opportunity to reinforce the client's fledgling attempts at emotion expression with feedback that supports his new behaviors. A therapist can provide reinforcement and support instead of punishment and derision for the man who expresses feelings such as, "I need to be close," "I'm lonely," or "I'm feeling overwhelmed and I need your help." (p. 8)

THE "STUFF" OF TRADITIONAL THERAPY

Boldly stated, just about all aspects of standard therapeutic culture dictate that it will not be a comfortable milieu for traditional men and boys. Traditional therapy, as defined by Sue, Sue, Neville, and Smith (2019) relies on "generic characteristics of counseling" (p. 427). Most therapy is "talk therapy," forcing the client into verbal communication in Standard English, which is not a male's strong suit.

Further, this therapy is individual centered. Verbal, emotional, and behavioral expressiveness are often prized, and client-therapist communication is the vehicle through which change is promoted. Openness and intimacy are valued as part of the therapeutic culture, as are a cause-effect orientation and a proclivity for setting long-range goals. Generally, individual sessions are fifty minutes in duration and take place in a therapist's office. A clear distinction between mental and physical well-being is predominant, and increased self-disclosure is seen as a mark of growth (Sue, 2010).

Brooks (1998) depicts the myriad ways in which there is a mismatch between the demands of psychotherapy and the demands of masculinity, as traditional men understand it. Typical psychotherapy includes expressing vulnerable feelings, nonsexual intimacy, loss of control, confronting pain, showing weakness or acknowledging failure, and seeking help—among other things. These stances fly in the face of a masculinity defined by strength, power, control, denial, self-reliance, and stoicism (Brooks, 1998).

This lack of goodness of fit plays out in the way that men bring to the therapeutic situation the baggage of their gender role socialization. Raised on competition and hierarchical ranking, "therapy seems an annoying distraction. Just as a pit stop causes a race car driver to lose precious laps, therapy takes time that could be used to perpetuate one's competitive advantage. Furthermore, there is no guarantee that therapy will enhance performance in any appreciable way" (Brooks, 1998, p. 45). Given that men usually arrive at therapy under duress, pressured by others, they already perceive therapy as a form of coercion to be resisted.

Men are socialized to be competent, so they tend to view anyone who needs therapy as someone who is less than competent, who can't solve his own problems. Additionally, since "two primary foci of masculinity are to be unlike women and to be in control" (Brooks, 1998, p. 50), needing therapy implies that a man's identity is shaken to the very core. Levant (1995) goes so far as to say that men suffer from what he calls "alexithymia" (p. 238), a state in which men actually are unaware of their feelings. Lacking this emotional awareness, when asked to identify their feelings, they "tend to rely on their cognition and try to logically deduce how they should feel. They cannot do what is so automatic for most women—simply sense inwardly, feel the feeling, and let the verbal description come to mind" (Levant, 1995, p. 239). Because men are socialized to be inexpressive and devalue emotion, this is a tremendous challenge to the therapist treating men and boys.

An offshoot of socialization to alexithymia is an aversion to the staples of traditional therapy such as talking, establishing connections, validating the personal experiences of others, and forming intimate relationships. Interpersonal encounters for men should be purpose-driven, involve problem solving, and have a tangible outcome (Brooks, 1998). Another reason that therapy is so uncomfortable is that men are brought up to confuse intimacy with sexuality and thus construct their friendships and relationships differently from women's.

The institution of psychotherapy has been "designed and conducted primarily by men but directed primarily at women" (Brooks, 1998, p. 42); thus, it is an institution to be avoided unless it is a last resort. Men usually arrive at traditional therapy only if it mandated legally, or if they face loss—of their partners, their sexual functioning, their jobs, or the like. An external impetus, rather than an intrinsic motivation, almost always drives men to the therapist's office.

Boys inherit negative attitudes about help-seeking through the boy code, and these attitudes are reinforced by cultural images of weakness if one has problems in the emotional or mental health domain (Kastner, 2018). Significant men in their lives may also, subtly or not-so-subtly, express opinions about those who are in counseling. Boys frequently are mandated to counseling in school settings for disruptive behavior, attention disorders, or aggression toward others; outside of the schoolyard, their mandates may come from parents who cannot "handle" behaviors such as oppositional defiance disorder, or in severe cases, from the juvenile justice system (Fazel, Hoagwood, Stephan, and Ford, 2014).

Finding or constructing activities, settings, and therapeutic relationships that enhance boy's and men's health and well-being is not an easy task, given the aforementioned challenges, yet there are some new models and practices that hold promise for bolstering their physical, mental, and emotional states and addressing problems if they do arise.

THEMES THAT ARE IMPORTANT TO MALE THERAPY

A savvy therapist can reach men by beginning with a recognition of the ways in which men and boys are socialized to be poor candidates for traditional therapy (Englar-Carlson, Evans, and Duffey, 2014). Among the many themes that must be understood are violence, relationships with women, relationships with other men, and fathering (Brooks, 1998). Unfortunately, violence in our society is seen as the "crucible of manhood [that separates] real men and boys [from] women and wimps" (Brooks, 1998, p. 16). Socially sanctioned violence for men is encouraged in such arenas as organized sports, hunting, and the military.

Normative male socialization and the social construction of masculinity predispose men to suffer from what Brooks (1995) terms the "centerfold syndrome." In a book of the same title, Brooks (1995) chronicles its development and describes its underlying expressions. Brooks outlines this major maladaptive syndrome common among contemporary American men.

There are five major elements to this syndrome: (1) voyeurism, (2) objectification, (3) the need for validation, (4) trophyism, and (5) the fear of true intimacy (Brooks, 1995). Men suffering from the syndrome are stunted in their growth toward authentic relations with women and in many ways are doomed to see themselves as failures as they navigate the life cycle. Voyeurism refers to the major role that visual stimulation plays in men's sexual responsiveness. Playing upon men's visual sense, the media and advertising bombard men with images of women—naked, semi-naked, in suggestive poses. As Brooks (1995) states, only religious fundamentalists and radical feminists seem concerned about this.

Objectification is closely linked to voyeurism, since men are the observers and women the observed. The women presented as images of the centerfold fantasy have their desired features highlighted (and often augmented, made over, touched up) so that men are viewing something highly coveted, but essentially unreal (Brooks, 1995). Women's true bodies, suffering the imperfections that age, childbirth, and real life bring, cannot ever measure up to this perfection, and thus men are engaged in sexual fantasy about something inaccessible and unreal, while missing out on opportunities for true intimacy with actual women (Brooks, 1995).

Men need the validation of others to shore up their flagging sense of contemporary manhood. Sex with women—particularly attractive ones—is one such means of validation; however, this gives tremendous status and power to women, and this is threatening to men (Brooks, 1995). Trophyism relates to this need for validation, so men compete for women's bodies and looks, and show off the spoils of their victories, to other men (Brooks, 1995). This competition is fierce, and it begins in adolescence. For centerfold syndrome-men, this competition continues throughout the life cycle, but just as trophies can be won, they can be lost or they can age, thus spurring men to seek newer, younger models to show off (Brooks, 1995).

Socialized to feel shame because of feelings of weakness, vulnerability, or need for another, even young boys suppress their need for connection, substituting instead their perceived need for sex and sexual conquest (Brooks, 1995). As primacy is given to satisfying sexual needs, boys', and later men's, connection or intimacy needs are suppressed and their communication skills atrophy.

There are various excuses given for the normalcy of the centerfold syndrome to include religion, nature, and survival of the fittest; yet, Brooks (1995) debunks these, finding that it is the social construction of masculinity and male sexual behavior that is to blame. The changing status of women in our society further threatens the status quo for men, lessening their power and control over women. Such a shift causes confusion, anger, and psychic pain for men (Englar-Carlson et al., 2014).

Brooks (1995) urges compassion for such men if one is to help them change and heal. In most cases, such men are not conscious of the root causes of their behavior and need to work through the strategies he outlines in a new psychotherapy for traditional men (1998) in order to become aware enough of socialization patterns that there is hope for change. Men's relationships with each other fare no better in a largely homophobic society (Bergman, 1995; Brooks, 1998; Pittman, 1993). As Brooks (1998) notes,

> Because men are raised to believe that masculinity is not innate but needs to be "proven," men tend to structure interactions with other men as challenges and contests. Intimacy between men is difficult, partially because it requires the admission of vulnerability, which risks the loss of the competitive edge. Additionally, because men so frequently connect intimacy with sexuality, strong emotional feelings for another man provoke an intense fear of homosexuality. (p. 20)

Fathering is an activity in which most traditional men suffer skills deficits because men are not socialized to nurturing roles (Brooks, 1998; Levant,

1995; Osherson, 1986; Pollack, 1995). What little guidance they do receive via the traditional model of fathering tells them to "toughen up" their boys because they do not want to raise "soft" sons. This predisposes men to early, and sometimes brutally wrenching, emotional separation from their sons, the withholding of physical affection, and the transmittal of information on what it means to be a "real man" (Osherson, 1986). Further, our social institutions do not promote active father engagement, even for those men who wish to be intimately involved in the birthing and raising of their boys.

There are other themes that may be important to recognize when thinking about creating effective interventions with men. Among these themes are emotions (fear, shame, pride, strength), roles (the dark shadow self, warrior), existential crises (loneliness, death), and relationships (Rabinowitz, 2005; 2014). Eichenfield (1996) adds dominance, power issues with other men (usually bosses and fathers), substance use and abuse, and anger at women as "consistent themes that were brought to the forefront" (p. 89) in the men's groups that he ran. The value of theme work is that it lessens men's shame over struggling with these issues and solidifies a sense of commonality among male members.

THERAPIES THAT WORK

Greer (2005) notes that not only are men less likely to seek therapy than are women, but even when they do end up in a therapist's office, they are less likely to be willing to engage. Socialization to what Levant (1995) refers to as normative male alexithymia means that "some men have difficulty identifying emotional problems because some norms for masculinity require their emotional lives to remain a mystery to them" (Adis, as cited in Greer, 2005, p. 62). Cited are examples of masculinity norms such as the widely held notion that men should hide their emotions and soldier on in the face of difficulty without acknowledging their struggles (Greer, 2005). Norms also dictate that men should always be in control and avoid too much intimacy, particularly with other men, two rules that can run counter to psychotherapy (Greer, 2005, p. 62).

Further, since men are less comfortable seeking help, when they finally do, their problems may be tremendously exacerbated. Indeed, in therapy, the standard question, "How does that make you feel" can draw puzzled looks from even mildly alexithymic male clients (Greer, 2005). That means when men do seek therapy, they could be really suffering (Kilmarten, as cited in Greer, 2005). "It's hard enough for the traditionally gendered men to ask for directions when they are lost in the car, so it's difficult for them to ask for help in any way," he says. "When they actually do get in the room, the typical man has to be in an incredibly deep level of pain" (Greer, 2005, p. 3).

Greer (2005) summarizes some of the suggestions of therapists who have had success working with male clients. Using a phenomenological approach, therapists should construct their personal definition of masculinity and how they experience that definition in daily life to avoid stereotyping men (Greer, 2005). Such self-definition may include seemingly atypical responses to gender, race, ethnicity, age, or the like.

Second, Greer (2005) urges others to "be an ear before being a therapist" (p. 4) that is, to be a respectful listener, demonstrate an understanding of and empathy for the conditions of contemporary manhood, and model the process as a problem-solving one; however, it is crucial that the therapist ultimately play the role of therapist, challenging men to see their role in ineffective or destructive behavior without ever demolishing their self-esteem.

Greer (2005) suggests making the office "masculine congruent" or gender neutral. Privacy and credibility (displaying credentials) assist men in feeling comfortable, as does the right choice of language (avoiding medical language that implies failure to men). Words such as "patient" or even "psychotherapy" themselves can alienate and shame men (Greer, 2005). Men also need to be educated about the very process of therapy itself; therefore, the therapist should spend time early clarifying how it works and answering questions (Englar-Carlson et al., 2014).

Men have very different styles to be accommodated in therapy; for example, traditional men may prefer more active sessions, with more "male friendly" techniques, such as sharing a bite to eat, shooting basketballs, watching a video, or assigning problem-solving "homework" (Englar-Carlson et al., 2014).

Greer (2005) notes that men do have "communicative strengths," but that they are different from women's. Men are socialized to be storytellers, so therapists should "get the guy to tell you a story about something that's happened to him. Start to look for emotional themes in the stories, highlight them and use emotional vocabulary to start a discussion about the themes" (Greer, 2005, p. 5). This approach assists men in overcoming alexithymia and learning a language for their associated psychological sensations; yet, it is a slow learning process, so patience on the therapist's part is crucial (Greer, 2005).

The major problem facing traditional therapists is that individual therapy forces men into interpersonal situations that men are not socialized to and, more often than not, that leads them into feelings of shame, fear, and denial when they are thrust into the unfamiliar role of asking for help (Rabinowitz, 2005; 2014). The male code creates barriers to men helping each other because it socializes men to fear intimacy, to detach from feelings of vulnerability, to idealize autonomy, and to hold a homophobic fear of male closeness (Brooks, 1998).

Group therapy might be the most natural vehicle for successfully reaching and treating the traditional male (Brooks, 1998). A working group will accommodate the "good old boy sociability style" (Farr as cited in Brooks, 1998, p. 86). Such a group is formed and carried out in a way that allows the male participants to avoid admitting that they are a prescribed group at all, or even that therapy is going on. Among the key elements of such a group are indirect norms, rather than those that directly confront traditional therapy.

First sessions are topic oriented and are conducted in a breezy, conversational style. Members are always organized around some sort of purpose, which is never defined as interpersonal contact; such a definition is antithetical to male culture, as it would imply the need for emotional attachment among men (Brooks, 1998; Rabinowitz, 2014). Food, drink, and activity are often used as the excuse for gathering. The mode of expression is predominantly storytelling, in testimonial fashion and teasing is permitted, although mutual support is implied in such teasing (Brooks, 1998). Personal contact among group members is indirect, with confrontations avoided and disclosure that is uncomfortable to other group members deflected—again, often with humor. Group members are sensitive to keeping appropriate psychic distance from others to avoid treading on their emotional space (Brooks, 1998).

Rabinowitz (2005; 2014) notes that men's groups are preferable because men share social and relational styles. The social persona that men must portray in the adult world of work and providing for their families is understood, so that men's disclosures can be loosened in the group. As men are "action" rather than "talk" oriented, they are comfortable with each other in group therapy modes that appear to be problem-solving in nature. Men can grow through the testimony of other men who have overcome difficulties as they can learn from them skills to better deal with interpersonal conflicts (Rabinowitz, 2014). With other men, clients can experience emotional safety in which to learn the "language" to express emotions, and learn it they must, as there are no women to assume that role. Men also may feel safer to express the "existential issues" (Rabinowitz, 2005, p. 268) that must be overcome in order to change.

In order to establish an effective men's group, one must consider the nature of the participants, unless this is a mandated group. Rabinowitz (2005; 2014) suggests that recruitment occurs through male contacts in the community and recommends that potential members be interviewed to see if they are a good fit and that there is commonality of purpose. Brooks (1998) offers criteria for selecting participants to include that they must be experiencing some degree of distress; they must be willing to consider changing aspects of their lifestyle; and they must be able to accept responsibility for making both the necessary changes and the sacrifices that always accompany it.

The Group Leader

Undoubtedly, the most important component of the group is its leader. The attitude that the leader holds toward traditional men is crucial, and his/her stance must embody empathy for their life experiences (Rabinowitz, 2014). The ability to deal with countertransference issues as well as a high degree of self-awareness as it relates to personal values, biases, and stereotypes, is essential to the well-functioning group. Brooks (1998) agrees, writing that in addition to being comfortable with men's relational and conversational styles, effective therapists must value, or at least empathize with traditional men, and must be able to help them see themselves in a larger context in what is called "gender-aware psychotherapy" (p. 83).

Brooks (2017) has extended his work on counseling boys and men by arguing that therapies must be modified to be less threatening and more in tune with the way males connect and feel comfortable expressing themselves. He argues that if boys and men are not comfortable going to therapists' offices, then counselors must move their practice outside of their office walls and into men's everyday lives.

Brooks (2017) touts the possibilities of primary prevention, psychoeducation, stage of change, consultation, and consciousness-raising alternatives because all can take place outside of the traditional office setting. Primary prevention programs are those that intentionally target specific groups to promote healthier functioning among their members. Their activities and curriculum also build emotional and relational competence.

When designing such programs for boys and young men, the focus should be on preventing likely problems and their corollary issues, bolstering the well-being assets that exist, and boosting prosocial well-being within each population (Brooks, 2017). While individual programs share these common goals, the actual programs themselves are created to reflect the uniqueness of the group of boys identified in terms of such variables as age, culture, ethnicity, and risk and protective factors (Rabinowitz, 2014).

Pollack (2005) urges therapists working with traditional men and boys not to put demands on them before they can handle them. The effective therapist, he argues, must be able to promote the "illusion of self-sufficiency [in the male client and must be able to tolerate a] stable transference constellation" (Pollack, 2005, p. 210) until issues can be interpreted from the man's own perspective. The therapist should help his male client solve concrete problems at hand, while developing rapport before verbally describing, interpreting, and/or confronting his behavior. Even after building rapport, it is best to have a trial run to see if the client is ready to link present masked struggles with earlier traumas (Pollack, 2005).

Prochaska and DiClemente's (1982) stages of change model states that most men and boys arrive at any counseling setting in the precontemplation stage, unaware of their need for change. If they are not ready to take on the change process, they most likely will act out with resistance and any change they do make will be surface at best. When thinking of the situations that most likely land boys in counseling, such as disciplinary problems in school or at home, or brushes with the juvenile justice system, it is no wonder that they come to counseling with negative attitudes or, at the very least, fear, hesitation, or little desire to modify what they perceive as their masculinity (Prochaska and DiClemente, 1982).

Prochaska and DiClemente (1982) cite both assets and liabilities of groups run by male or female therapists. On the other hand, as Brooks (1998) argues, simply being a man does not make one empathetic to traditional men; as Sue, Sue, Neville, and Smith (2012) note, counselors often are more comfortable with middle- and upper-class modes of being by virtue of their upbringing and/or education and training. Class sensitivity is essential in effectively dealing with the pain of traditional men and boys.

Many men themselves may be the victims of "restrictive early socialization and hypermasculinity" (Brooks, 1998, p. 149). On the other hand, female group leaders may be experienced as "the other" and they may be perceived as having a higher degree of empathy or relied upon unconsciously to provide the "language" for men's emotions. They can be successful leading men's groups if they are skilled at bridging the gender and cultural differences and can comfortably understand and navigate in the terrain of traditional men's communication styles and metaphors. They also must appreciate men's fears of emotional closeness and expression since women are more apt to be socialized to a model of self-in-relation (Brooks, 1998). Above all else, kinship seems to be the crucial component of good therapy.

There are undoubtedly powerful roles in men's lives for female therapists (Erickson, 1993). Drawing from descriptions and transcriptions of the case histories of the author's work as a psychotherapist with male patients, Erickson (1993) promotes a vision of an intuitive yet research-supported successful female therapist. The many case examples Erickson (1993) uses are males who went to her office for a variety of needs, either alone or in tandem with a female partner, who made breakthroughs in understanding through specific techniques.

Erickson (1993) describes her approach as "psychodynamic" with an emphasis on uncovering the male client's unconscious problems with himself and within his family of origin's collective practices. Because the field has seen the influx of so many more women as practitioners, females' impact on males and their emotional lives is important to the current state of the field. Erickson (1993) cautions that producing change for men is a difficult task, necessitating a change in their worldview that demands a sophisticated reliance on both traditional female virtues of warmth and nurturing and the inculcation of traditional male roles of leadership and accomplishment focus.

Although it is vital for a female therapist to have an affinity for men, this orientation can be developed by heterosexual or homosexual female therapists and can be the subject of preparatory study and work. The typical male client will have difficulty with either intimate feelings or aggressive impulses; however, the female therapist will seek to embody the holding environment that will allow the past of the family of origin's pain to be revealed (Erickson, 1993). This is performed through an initial display of confident communication by the therapist, who sets the boundaries, physical nature, and structure of the sessions. When male anger arises subsequently, it must be met with adequate understanding and reaction.

In covering the primary terms of transference and countertransference, Erickson (1993) advises the female therapist to develop her own unique style, but that it must be arrived at through hard work of supervised practice, intensive reflection, and collegial discussion. In managing transference, the female therapist will usually need to adjust the male client's need to detect credibility in her.

Methods to gain credibility include speaking the male language, initiating the use of endearments, and bringing forth the client's realization that sexuality will be present in his interactions with the therapist, though strictly not possible as therapeutic practice (Erickson, 1993). The therapist becomes the authority limiting the male abuse of power while coaxing the gentler, tender emotions out from behind their defenses. There will be occasions of boundary violations that need to be managed while not denying or repressing the personal reactions between client and therapist.

In discussion treatment planning, Erickson (1993) highlights the need for the female therapist to develop the gift of improvisation, which will lead the treatment into more emotional, rather than strictly cognitive areas. In a more pragmatic sense, female therapists must be fully grounded in the male socialization patterns and common developmental arrests of her male clients. Rather than focusing only on the present symptoms of the crisis, treatment for either married couples or individual males should be ready to examine the family of origin's continued hindrance of the male's acceptance of the good-enough view of his past. In the technique of redecision therapy, the male client is brought back through regression to a defining earlier moment in his life when a debilitating consequential decision was arrived at, to be finally understood and re-evaluated (Erickson, 1993; Goulding and Goulding, 1997).

To generate developmental growth in the client, the therapist must have embarked on a rigorous examination of her own path. Erickson (1993) notes that her methods are not suitable for the quick-fix approach, and normally require three years or so of sessions, slightly longer for those with less cognitive firepower. In order to produce the more desirable result of second order-change, where men change the basic structures of their interior lives, meaningful connection must be established between the female and male languages.

The therapist must elicit awareness in her clients of necessary areas for choice, performed by the client and not by the therapist, by introducing only the right amount of disequilibrium in the encounters (Erickson, 1993). To perform this work in therapy, the female therapist should know developmental theory in order to formulate longer term goals. She should operate at a higher developmental level than the client, to be able to instruct through modeling as well as verbal technique (Erickson, 1993).

Erickson (1993) further defines her approach as systems thinking, in which the client's problems are positioned in the larger contexts of family of origin, socialization patterns, and current family and relationship pressures. The therapist must resist the temptation for the male client to reflexively blame all others to the exclusion of the self, or to blame the self exclusively. If larger connections can be established, the male client can develop a sense of hope, or locate resources of inner strength; thus, forging better lives both for himself and for others within his social network (Erickson, 1993).

A common barrier to this achievement is the unresolved need of men to have an enduring bond with their fathers. This loss can be felt by daughters as well as sons, yet often results in emotionally deprived men. If therapists have a "father hunger" or unresolved feelings of other loss, they may be recalcitrant in exploring their clients' problem areas of loss. Through clinical examples, Erickson (1993) demonstrates common curative practices that can be established with males in individual therapy.

In couple's therapy, the colorings of a habitual feminist perspective can lead female therapists to side with the wife against the husband. Using systems thinking, female therapists can put into practice a strong affiliation with the rights and dilemmas of both sexes. Erickson (1993) concludes that men and women have similar needs for friendship and intimacy, but different ways of expressing them.

These conflicts can be exacerbated in two different models of men's groups and family of origin extended sessions. Though Erickson (1993) describes successful practices in both, she summarizes the dangers in each with caveats against rigid or deterministic interventions that do not aim to shape men's lives into confluence with women's.

In summary, male or female, a good men's group leader is confident, can take charge, and is empathetic. The group leader should be genuine, caring, and knowledgeable, while not tolerating inappropriate behavior in the group. Strong, but not authoritarian, this person models what s/he seeks in the client's group (Brooks, 1998).

Effective Men's Groups

There are issues that one must keep in mind in developing a men's group that works. First, there is the need to take a transgenerational focus—that is, to see each man's history in the context of his family background and socialization (Brooks, 1998). This allows participants to understand the roots of their beliefs, values, and behaviors. Next, the group's work should be cast in the light of a journey (Rabinowitz, 2005). A particularly useful activity for men, especially those in mid-life, is the gender-role journey that relies on the use of metaphors to stimulate self-examination (O'Neil, 2015).

Most traditional men have repertoires of highly sex-typed behaviors that restrict the development of "truly full human identity" (O'Neil and Egan, 1992, p. 109). Additionally, they are very invested in these long-held behaviors and will be loath to examine them too critically, let alone cast them off for new ones; thus, the gender-role journey metaphor is a vehicle for thinking about one's socialization and the roles that sexism may have held in the socialization process (O'Neil, 2015). The journey conceptualization allows men to reflect on previous experiences, evaluate them and then discard, modify, or retain them based on their usefulness to them at this time in their lives (O'Neil and Egan, 1992).

Men must be engaged in "befriending the darkness and pain" (O'Neil and Egan, 1992, p. 112) before healing can occur. Emboldened by the support of other group members, men may move through a five-phase process. The first step is to engage in psychoeducational exploration of how one's gender role stereotypes were learned and reinforced in the first place. Within the safety of the group, a man may be surprised to find that he is not alone in feeling the weight of the social impress to "become a man" at the expense of vulnerable, but necessary emotions (O'Neil and Egan, 1992).

The second and third phases, which can be facilitated by exercises, creative problem solving, and role play within the group, engage members in confronting their fears of change, articulating new role variations that are desirable to them, and strategizing about how to move into those new roles (O'Neil and Egan, 1992). Further, positive use of anger to buoy men through their change process is discussed; this is a critical dialogue, since men's anger so often leads them to feelings of hopelessness or depression. The final two stages, how to channel anger into activism and individual growth, and how to motivate others to do the same, may be other offshoots of the group's journey (O'Neil and Egan, 1992).

The gender role journey is a good example of a means to evoking men's emotional pain—a necessary outcome of a successful men's group, Brooks argues (1998). From a young age, boys are socialized not to show emotion, and may not even be aware of feeling certain emotions and pain that may be buried deep in adult males. It must be evoked, expressed, and rechanneled if men are to heal (O'Neil, 2015). This cannot occur if men do not feel safe and validated in the group, if they are not excited to be forming connections with others who share similar troubles, and if they do not see the therapist as benevolent (Brooks, 1998).

The all-male group needs to learn to view any issue as one that affects all men, rather than as the pathological expression of an individual man's problem. This is what Yalom and Leszcz (2005) term "universality" within a group, and it serves as the foundation for recognizing one's connectedness to others. Across the void, men can reach out and form friendships, rather than feeling the need to compete with one another. In the absence of hierarchical comparison and competition, the possibility for intimacy among men is increased (Yalom and Leszcz, 2005). This is a huge triumph in the face of traditional men's socialization.

A men's group also can help to decentralize the role that women play in men's lives (Brooks, 1998). This is linked to the above-mentioned formation of wider friendship networks among men, since wives or female partners so often are the only emotional support that men have. The lack of women in the group forces men into uncomfortable new territory; they cannot fall back on women to express or translate their emotions for or provide the nurturing, so they must learn these skills in relation to each other.

Men also must learn a new way of speaking with each other. Male conversational styles tend to be permeated with self-listening that is, not truly listening to another man, but focusing, instead, on what one wants to say, and jumping in to discuss one's own experience rather than appreciating the other's. Rather than active listening, men are engaged in active preparation for inserting themselves into the speaker's dialogue. Men also are apt to "report talk [rather than] rapport talk" (Brooks, 1998, p. 115).

As men learn to listen, they are likely drawn to the testimonials of other men. Brooks (1998) suggests having veteran members return to the group to share testimonials and discuss their progress on the gender role journey. Within the group experience, members need to withhold their desire to advise others and simply be present to them. This is difficult, as men are socialized to see giving advice to others as a mode of expressing caring. Their being drawn to problem-solving often makes them impatient with simply listening, so part of the group process is learning to value listening to problems that may not have solutions in order to bear witness to another man's pain (O'Neil, 2015).

As men in the group learn to listen, even to painful stories from their colleagues, they promote greater and greater self-disclosure among men, which is a sequential process (Yalom and Leszcz, 2005). It is extremely helpful if the group leader models this behavior through timely and appropriate self-disclosure on his/her part. Structure in the group sessions is important to the group's successful functioning. As mentioned previously, men like clarity about all aspects of the group process and individual sessions because "many men are uncomfortable with structureless situations" (Rabinowitz, 2005, p. 273). A clear purpose for activities is consonant with their socialization to work. Theme work provides some of that clarity and reinforces commonality of experience among men.

Brooks (1998) views the major themes in traditional men's lives as work, violence, relationships with women, relationships with other men, fatherhood, and health. Briefly put, men's socialization puts them at risk in each of these areas. First, they grow up learning to identify self with work; in the blue-collar world, in a changing economy, this sense of self-through-work is tenuous. Second, they are brought up to suppress the needy or vulnerable emotions, but are given license to express themselves through competition, anger, and violence in arenas such as sports, hunting, and military experiences (O'Neil, 2015).

Third, men have a love-hate relationship with the women in their lives because they fear and need them, yet resent those very facts (Brooks, 1998). Male to male expressions of intimacy are taboo, unless ritually enacted in the aforementioned arenas, as they are seen to be tantamount to homosexual behavior. Contemporary men also are challenged in fathering because, on one hand, there is a popular sentiment that men should be more engaged in fathering their children, but on the other hand, there are few, if any, mentors or role models available to men to show them how to do this effectively (Brooks, 1998; O'Neil, 2015). Finally, men are socialized to "tough it out," thereby ignoring even serious medical or mental health issues in favor of "being a man" about their health.

The effective group leader will attempt to strengthen relationships within the group as well as provide psychoeducation that illustrates the commonality among men through themes (Brooks, 1998; Philpot, Brooks, Lusterman, and Nutt, 1997). When appropriate, the leader can even suggest outside reading to further participants' education.

Humor, accessible language, and metaphors are essential in helping men to identify the dominant issues and how they play out in their lives. Using the active, problem-solving model, the group can assist individuals in strategizing solutions to the concrete problems they are experiencing while building trust to tackle their root causes. Each small behavioral change needs to be praised, even if the leader must choose only a best approximation of the desired behavior (Brooks, 1998).

EFFECTIVE THERAPY FOR BOYS AND ADOLESCENT MALES

While interest in men's groups as an effective treatment mode for traditional men has been growing, it is only recently that the profession has thought more seriously about applying the tenets of successful work with men to work with boys. Levant (2005) articulates the two major crises of boyhood that lie behind the issues that boys reluctantly may bring to counseling. In fact, these crises are likely to be missed because we expect boys to be self-sufficient and to keep things to themselves.

The first is what he terms "school daze"—when boys arrive at school much less ready than girls to adapt to its environment and behavioral expectations. Boys are "twice as likely to be diagnosed with learning disabilities, five times more likely to have conduct disorders, six times as likely to be classified as special needs" (Levant, 2005, p. 162). Boys are shaped to move away from their greater emotionality at birth, and are encouraged to be less expressive, unless that expression is one of anger. The masculine code dictates that they be wary of emotional expression and vulnerability (Moon, 2018).

A second crisis arrives in adolescence. Boys have a difficult time finding direction at this point in time because they often have problematic relationships with their fathers; fathers view their primary roles as enforcing the boy code, fathers often are emotionally and/or geographically distant, and fathers often are preoccupied with their provider roles (Moon, 2018). The adult male also may be experiencing the strains of entering midlife and turn inward at the very time that their sons need them most.

Since adolescent boys are supposed to be always ready for sex and avoidant of anything that smacks of being feminine, they are cut off from the emotional/expressive side of themselves (Vernon and Schimmel, 2018). There is a deep shame in feeling any of the emotions that derive from that part of their being, and this shame is often masked with substance abuse and risky behavior. Kiselica (2005) takes issue with Levant (2005) and others, however, finding no empirical evidence that boys are more apt to suffer from alexithymia; such a view, he fears, predisposes therapists to perceive boys as being resistant or disengaged therapeutically. The problem may lie in the mode of therapy.

Male-friendly counseling with such boys must consider their preferred styles (Kiselica, 2005). Like men, boys gravitate toward groups that are engaged in activity; therefore, they need professional counselors who are willing to be participatory and to move their therapy into new venues (Vernon and Schimmel, 2018). What many counselors misinterpret as resistance to therapy is actually men's discomfort with traditional styles of therapy (Kiselica, 2005).

Drawing from empirical research and his practice with teen fathers, Kiselica (2005) found several common components of effective group therapy for boys. Reexamining the traditional fifty-minute session and the formal setting, is a first step.

Traditional boys tend to develop trusting relationships with their friends over time, by changing out, doing things together, and gradually letting others into their psychic world. Consequently, they are a bit like fish out of water when they are thrust into formal counseling settings in which they are expected to remain seated and spill their guts for an hour at a time once a week. (Kiselica, 2005, p. 20)

Humor and self-disclosure must first be modeled by the therapist. It is vital to place primary emphasis on helping boys focus on their most pressing concerns rather than asking open-ended questions such as "How are you feeling?" Boys must be treated professionally and observe the type of availability in time and manner that demonstrate that the therapist is someone to be trusted (Vernon and Schimmel, 2018). It is also important that the therapist explore the boys' own views about counseling.

Programs for Boys

Counseling programs for boys must adhere to boy-friendly educational principles and content if they are to be successful. Psycho-educational offerings that are boy-friendly hold certain techniques in common that include:

- lessons that produced products
- learning that is structured as a game
- sessions that require a high level of motor activity
- lessons that ask boys to be responsible for promoting others' learning; activities that are aimed at solving problems
- lessons that require both teamwork and competition
- learning activities that are focused on boys' personal realization (such as defining their masculinity, their values, their present and future social roles)
- activities built upon novelty and surprise (Reichert and Hawley, 2010)

Gurian (2001) remarks that boys tend to use up more space as they are learning, especially when they are younger. Their spatial brains, he notes, make it necessary for them to spread out work and use all of the space available to them as they learn. Movement helps to stimulate their brains; it also acts to get impulsive behavior under control, therefore using activities that allow them to manipulate objects lowers fidgeting, and likely helps to lower levels of serotonin and higher metabolisms (Gurian, 2001).

A concept that is particularly critical to counseling programs for boys is that cooperative learning appears to come more naturally to girls, as they are better able to attend to codes of social interaction in a group setting. Boys are more likely to focus their energies on doing the task at hand well and are therefore less attuned to the emotions of their classmates. Boys also are highly sensitive to pecking orders in the classroom and are what Gurian (1997) calls "fragile learners" when they are on the low end of the order. This appears from brain research to be related to the higher level of cortisol released in the brains of low-status male learners. Cortisol, a stress hormone, has been shown to decrease learning as it forces boys to focus on survival instincts or "fight or flight" rather than higher-order cognitive learning (National Scientific Council on the Developing Child, 2014).

Lack of attention to the emotions of their classmates, pecking order, and cortisol levels mean that young participants in group counseling programs need to feel accepted as equal partners and may need some modeling as to how to be more sensitive to group dynamics (Vernon and Schimmel, 2018). Learning teams and group work benefit both genders, but boys are more likely to create highly structured teams and generally waste little time in choosing leaders. Boys in a group also will differ in preferred learning styles, so mixing them in learning teams helps bring a variety of approaches to a problem-solving situation and can teach respect for individual differences (Vernon and Schimmel, 2018).

Several exemplary school-based counseling programs are Building Champions (Miller, 2016) and Operation: Breaking the Boy Code (Moon, 2018). Each shares a belief that counselors can be instrumental in helping boys redefine masculinity in ways that promote well-being and prosocial behavior. The work in each program is conducted in groups with elementary school boys; groups are deliberately mixed with different personalities and school identity statuses (Miller, 2016; Moon, 2018). The programs rely a great deal on experiential learning, activities and movement, visual art and creative projects, story and legend, and rituals; yet they also have built-in pauses for guided reflection—a powerful part of any experiential learning.

Miller (2016) pauses boys to ask them to think about what happened, what it meant, and what they are going to do with the new insight gained. Miller's (2016) program is conducted with upper-elementary and middle school boys. Developed in line with the goals of the American School Counselors Association (2019), it asks boys to think about defining champions in ways that deviate from contemporary definitions of masculinity and heroism.

The program relies heavily on goal setting, using the SMART goal model (specific, measurable, achievable, relative, and timely) to assist boys in becoming more accountable, self-disciplined, and responsible (Miller, 2016). Every session focuses on a virtue, such as leadership, team work, positive mind-set, trust, personal values, fair play, integrity, and respect. Boys also craft personal definitions of courage and heroism that can play out in their own lives.

The program focuses on active learning and visual representations such as worksheets, interactive art projects, and literature as prompts. It models respect for diversity in that it asks participants to generate multiple ways of thinking about each key concept, such as the myriad ways one could demonstrate leadership, similar to UDL (Miller, 2016). From the rich array of possibilities, boys can locate expressions that have goodness of fit. The program also intentionally confronts negative stereotypes about masculinity, such as behaviors that are representative of a negative mindset, bias against others, or exclusion of those who are viewed as different (Miller, 2016).

Moon's (2018) Operation: Breaking the Boy Code is an eight-week program for boys in grades three to five. The genesis of the program came from observations the author made about the shift in boys' behavior toward her as they approached this developmental stage. Noting their earlier personalities as those filled with goals, hopes and dreams, a desire to help, and the willingness to be physically affectionate and emotionally expressive, Moon (2018) laments a visible change in boys in later grades:

> Family issues, finances, problems at home, divorce, learning difficulties and untimely deaths, begin to wear on their tiny souls. Academic, social and behavior problems begin to manifest. If these situations are not adequately addressed, the spark of hope starts to dim. I can actually see a physical tightening of the jaw muscles. They accept my hugs, but I have to initiate. I believe that these boys are incredibly frightened, worried, and confused. Since boys are not encouraged to talk about their feelings and concerns, they push that fear deep inside and put on "The Front." (p. 2)

Moon (2018) developed her program to combat "The Front," to break the mask that is the carefully controlled persona that boys show the world. Program goals are to increase relational and communication skills, demonstrate a healthy range of masculinities, and use expressive therapy techniques to bolster self-esteem and increase individual self-reflection. The lessons have intriguing names to include the Boy Code Brotherhood, Knights of the Round Table, Wisdom of the Tribe, the League of Extraordinary Heroes, the Way of the Samurai, and the Magic Circle; and the program culminates with initiation rituals (Moon, 2018).

Moon (2018), like many other authors, believes that boys lack positive modern-day heroes as well as the rites of passage and rituals of many other cultures; thus, the curriculum uses activities involving stories and myths, role play, codes and signs, totems and symbols, artwork, and comics and cartoons. In identifying real superheroes of contemporary society and helping boys define what superpowers they possess and can use to positively impact the world, the program leads them to confront problems such as bullying, stereotyping, and stigmatizing others (Moon, 2018).

At the completion of the program, boys enter the Boy Code Brotherhood (Moon, 2018). Each is tapped to become a member through rituals that reveal the secrets of the group's crest, the motto, and the group signals. Unlike some programs that do not use arts and crafts with boys—seeing those as the stuff of girls' groups—Moon (2018) relies heavily on the expressive arts in ways that hark back to mythical shields, totem animals, American Indian tribal art, and samurai warrior symbols, reclaiming these modes of identification and expression for boys.

Adventure Therapy or Experiential Therapy

Adventure-based counseling (ABC) is a good match for boys and adolescent males who, according to Portrie-Bethke, Christian, Brown, and Hill (2012), are the most challenging population to counsel and the least well-suited for traditional talk therapy due to a high rate of comorbidity between behavioral problems and deficiency in language skills. Avoiding the heavy reliance on talking and shifting the focus to acting and then reflecting or analyzing is at the heart of ABC. The commonalities among all ABC programs, regardless of setting, are that they are action-oriented, involve risks (real or perceived or both), place an emphasis on metaphor, and show participants how to transfer what they have gleaned from their experiences to other settings such as school or home (Portrie-Bethke et al., 2012).

ABC harnesses natural male energy and encourages boys to seamlessly engage in therapy through confronting and mastering unfamiliar situations (Portrie-Bethke et al., 2012). Because they are forced to be out of their comfort zone, boys can't plan their responses and therefore are thrust into disequilibrium, which is necessary for change to occur. Once they have mastered the challenge, there is cathartic transformation that is aided by the counselors helping boys to process what they experienced and identify their strengths that can then be transferred to future situations (Portrie-Bethke et al., 2012).

ABC works because it is problem- or solution-focused and the counselor is seen as an embedded participant rather than an outsider trying to get inside the boys' heads (Portrie-Bethke et al., 2012). Astute counselors can perform informal assessments, both of individual and group mental health needs, and then plan activities and select dynamics to be processed after the activities. The format of ABC can be tailored to be anything from weekly sessions to lengthier retreats.

The curriculum can be applied in classroom settings; however, the preferred location is outdoors, as there are liberating aspects of natural settings, where boys can move more freely, exert themselves, and release frustrations and anxieties through those exertions (Portrie-Bethke et al., 2012). They are less able to hide or be inhibited in responding to their experiences and emotions, but skillful ABC leaders couch these in metaphoric language. In doing so, they frame activities as metaphors for what the boys experience in everyday life and suggest more appropriate or effective ways to deal with those problems (Portrie-Bethke et al., 2012).

Since boys, especially adolescents, are prone to risk-taking, the activities of ABC allow them to take socially appropriate risks that have natural consequences. As boys solve problems creatively during their challenges, they learn which solutions are efficacious—a valuable insight because those behaviors that are perceived as having efficacy are more likely to be used again in the future. Portrie-Bethke et al. (2012) note that "as adolescents successfully engage in ABC, they often experience gains in self-concept, increased internal locus of control, and elevated self-confidence" (p. 194).

Group therapy often is a necessity, particularly in schools, due to fiscal and time restraints. Fortunately, though, this mode capitalizes on boys' natural affinity for group interactions, particularly if recreational and educational activities are integrated into the so-called therapy; for example, informational recreational activities may help to diffuse tension about the content of a therapeutic session, and the educational aspect of the session may be more effectively delivered through a video and discussion, or a group problem-solving task (Vernon and Schimmel, 2018). Above all, therapists must be "active, involved mentors" (Kiselica, 2005, p. 25) if they are to reach their clients.

Group therapy may be a particularly valuable experience for boys and adolescent males sharing a common mental health challenge; for example, Horne and Kiselica (1999) and Spurgeon and Paredes (2012) promote group work and support with populations such as gay and questioning boys, those from single-parent homes, boys who have undergone loss, adoptees, teen fathers, adolescent sex offenders or other juvenile offenders, and those who have developmental delays or specific learning or emotional challenges. Each of their handbooks contains dedicated chapters on specific populations in terms of implications for effective counseling practice.

Culturally Responsive Programs

In response to the critical need for more and better mental health counseling for boys, several innovative programs have sprung up over time. Perez-Gualdron, Yeh, and Russell (2016) report on one such program called Boys II Men, developed for urban high school boys of color. The program focuses on five content areas to include social connections and support; school engagement; gender roles; identity; and planning for the future (Perez-Gualdron et al., 2016). A primary value of the program was that it was culturally responsive and involved ninth-grade boys transitioning into high school, because this is a typical dropping out point for males of color.

The authors believe that the overwhelmingly negative statistics about urban male students of color are directly linked to their marginalization throughout history, even to this day. The cultural strengths of such boys are often censored in order to maintain heterogeneous institutional values; therefore, this program deliberately brought to the forefront perceived cultural assets of these boys, such as their leadership abilities, collective orientation, and activism (Perez-Gualdron et al., 2016).

Barriers to young males of color seeking school or community counseling include gender role restrictions, lack of knowledge of services, and dearth of culturally competent practitioners. By making their program school-based, Boys II Men stood a better chance of drawing boys into an interactive counseling setting (Perez-Gualdron et al., 2016). To combat notions of masculinity as hinging on independence and "going it alone," the counselors build in activities that facilitate establishing social support and becoming fully engaged in the school community. The intent of the program is to help young men identify and strengthen positive coping skills to employ when faced with educational and social stress (Perez-Gualdron et al., 2016).

Perez-Gualdron et al. (2016) believe that one of the key strengths of this program lies in its consideration of masculine gender role norms and conflicts in the context of color; as the goal was to help the boys understand some of the emotional and physical risks involved in the boy code and how they can affect health and well-being now and in the future. The groups also dealt bluntly with the negative stereotypes and low expectations placed upon boys of color. Building relationships with positive role models outside of school was one important strategy as such role models and mentors have been proven to be protective buffers who also offer the boys glimpses of different paths outside of the more stereotypical ones, such as athlete or rap singer (Perez-Gualdron et al., 2016).

The participants themselves requested that work be done around the gang activity that was so prevalent in their communities. The facilitators helped them to understand the factors leading to gang participation and identify ways in which school and other forms of relationships and community engagement could fill some of the voids that gangs did (Perez-Gualdron et al., 2016). This involved confronting the very real fact that many boys of color do not feel welcome in our schools. The program worked to enhance relational aspects of the boys' learning to embed them in the life of the school and its members in more positive ways (Perez-Gualdron et al., 2016).

Because those who are marginalized and disengaged lack concrete and inspiring visions of their futures, it was important that the facilitators work with the students on articulating and goal-setting around future paths that extended beyond the aforementioned stereotypes for males of color (Perez-Gualdron et al., 2016). Making the connection between these dream goals and daily school-based activities bridged a gap and provided a rationale for greater academic and relational engagement.

The group work was based upon best practice principles for boys and adolescents; that is, the participants themselves helped to design the group content and procedures, the sessions were participatory in nature, and each group began with an icebreaker and then an activity (Perez-Gualdron et al., 2016). Qualitative interviews conducted by the researchers at the conclusion of the group indicated that the participants responded positively to the relational approach that fostered connections among the young men (Perez-Gualdron et al., 2016).

They built social networks in ways that often don't happen with marginalized populations. The open discussion of such topics as race, attitudes toward women, gang involvement, and navigating identities cemented the boys' commitment to the group as did building a future plan and tying it to specific school engagement practices (Perez-Gualdron et al., 2016).

In any group therapy setting a final consideration is the racial, ethnic, and religious make-up of the group members. Mental health interventions for discrete populations of males must shift from the traditional Eurocentric, symptom-based approach to one more grounded in specific cultural realities (Caldwell and White, 2005). Just as men must be seen in "cross-cultural" light, so, too, must the individual members of the group be appreciated in terms of their cultural backgrounds. Addressing their concerns in five essays, Caldwell and White (2005) argue that mental health interventions for discrete populations of males need to shift from a Eurocentric symptom-based approach to one grounded in specific cultural reality.

To promote therapists' self-awareness, there must be a development of working historical knowledge of the oppression, racism, and struggles of the diverse populations. Caldwell and White (2005) promote the process of self-examination for all therapists, white or African American, to probe for enforced stereotypical images of black men. They encourage breaking away from class-based inheritances by visiting black community events. Casas, Turner, and Ruiz de Esparza (2005) recommend integrating counseling sessions early in a Hispanic boy's life to overcome the cultural avoidance of counseling. Sue et al. (2012) steer the counseling of Asian men toward a cognitive therapy model that focuses on external issues of acculturation, rather than culturally disfavored self-exploration.

Although Halderman (2005) states that therapists of gay and bisexual men may come to feel that the diversity of their clients' experiences relegates the commonality of their sexual orientation as minor, discrimination and disapproval have shaped these men's core understanding of social relationships. Maples and Robertson (2005) indicate that religion would be a significant element of a patient's personal history, and this affiliation would likely impact counseling in the firmness of their religious beliefs, their views of gender and masculinity issues, and in their relation to religious hierarchy. The complexities of these variables in counseling cry out for a more inclusive, self-awareness focused preparation of novice practitioners in the helping fields.

Horne and Kiselica (1999) share how to counsel specific populations of boys and young males to include African American, Asian American, American Indian, Alaska Native American, and non-Hispanic white boys, pointing out both the commonalities in some aspects of therapy across these populations of males while highlighting aspects of cultural uniqueness that influence effective counseling. They also discuss the implications for counseling in terms of connections to the boys' families and other important community members, such as elders or leaders.

While it is impossible for one counselor to be completely knowledgeable and skilled in working with the diverse subpopulations of our multifaceted society, it is important to be as well-versed as possible, know how to find pertinent resources, and be open to learn from clients through asking open-ended questions and actively listening. With the concept of "cultural humility" replacing the earlier notion of "multicultural competence," the professional counselor will avail him or herself of opportunities to be a continuous learner in these areas (Hook, Davis, Owen, and DeBlaere, 2017).

In addition to the therapist's stance, actual programming developed around the specific needs and vulnerabilities of particular populations of boys needs to grow; however, the successful programs will be those that are assets-based, beginning with the strengths of different cultures. DeAngelis (2014), for example, writes on resilience-building work with African American boys in the wake of the shooting deaths of Michael Brown, Trayvon Martin, and Jordan Davis. Because black boys are so often negatively stereotyped and viewed, programs that help them develop resilience and positive racial and cultural identity are absolutely vital. This approach presumes that preventative, developmental approaches to boys' mental health will decrease the need for formal therapeutic interventions later (DeAngelis, 2014).

Gonzales (2016) conducted qualitative research on counseling groups for at-risk minority male youth and learned from adolescent interviewees the power of all-boys' groups that address the needs of a particular culture or community. These informants shared that the greatest need was in addressing issues of violence, including conflict resolution skills, violence protection techniques, and modification of behaviors that put themselves and their communities and families in harm's way (Gonzales, 2016). All participants expressed the value of therapeutic rapport, both with the therapist and with each other.

The conversational nature of their group, plus lots of activities that kept them moving, engaged in motivational interviewing, and having ownership in the group process, were cited by the boys as critical to remaining involved in the process and committed to group members (Gonzales, 2016). They valued both the group and individual formats for counseling and stressed how important it was that connections between what took place in group and school personnel were maintained so that there was awareness on the school's part of content and progress (Gonzales, 2016).

Schools are a particularly ripe ground for programs from active or arts therapy to restorative justice programs that develop empathy between perpetrator and victim and encourage dialogue and expression of emotions between them. There also are promising experiments with community-based preventative programs growing out of prosocial connections such as those found in faith groups and volunteer associations.

DeAngelis (2014) notes one fascinating program called SHAPE-UP in which barbers serve as unofficial mentors to boys of color, using the "freewheeling" kinds of discussions that take place in barber shops to engender discussion of hot topics such as violence or STDs. Like barbers, there are many "invisible" heroes and mentors in the community and in our schools who can bolster prosocial behavior and mental health in boys and young men.

Chapin (2015) studied resilience in Mexican American boys growing up in the United States, a group at high risk for negative outcomes in all domains of health. Through this study, it was determined that there were components of resilience that helped the boys to be successful; these components were both internal and external. One aspect was that the boys could identify their definition of positive life outcomes, which included being a good family man and a good provider (Chapin, 2015). Becoming a provider required their graduation from high school and college and being prepared for a good career path.

Chapin (2015) also found that the boys identified family and community relationships as critical to their success. These individuals helped them stay on track with their goals, were sounding boards and confidantes, and served as positive role models and mentors. As far as internal characteristics to which they attributed their resilience, self-regulation, self-confidence, and the ability to adapt to life circumstances were key (Chapin, 2015). Helping boys and young men identify the assets they have in themselves and in their lives, defining what success looks like for each individual, setting goals, and finding support systems are necessary parts of therapeutic and psychoeducational programs aimed at all males (Chapin, 2015).

Another short-term program that is low cost and developed for middle school boys is the Boy's Forum, which mainly has been used with Hispanic and African American boys (O'Neil, Challenger, Renzulli, Casper, and Webster, 2013). Few gender role interventions for this age exist and the Boy's Forum draws on psychosocial theory as well as research and literature on gender role transitions, multicultural formulations of masculinity, and prosocial behavior and well-being (O'Neil et al., 2013). The Boy's Forum presents research on the hazards of growing up male balanced with activities stressing positive modes of being male through empowerment, emotional awareness, and personal problem solving (O'Neil et al., 2013).

Group facilitators take advantage of media, group discussions, exercises that encourage youth empowerment, and judicious use of adult self-disclosure. The program was evaluated at its onset, immediately after its conclusion, and three weeks later. Most participants attending the Boy's Forum reported that the program had a positive impact on thinking, feelings, and to some extent, their behaviors during the three-week period after it ended (O'Neil et al., 2013).

The Therapeutic Effects of Mentoring

While the previously mentioned forms of more structured therapy and counseling have proved effective with boys and young men, it is clear that there also are therapeutic benefits of both formal and informal mentoring situations in which younger males take part, either in an individual or group relationship. Programs that are supported by empirical research results demonstrate that those involved in mentoring are more successful academically, graduate at higher rates, have higher levels of well-being and less involvement with substance abuse or physical violence, and are less likely to be gang members or interact with the juvenile justice system (Jarjoura, 2013).

The American Institute for Research highlights successful programs such as A Cut Above, which is run in the Harlem Children's Zone, and House of Umoja in Philadelphia, that operates on an African kinship model and aims to prevent gang violence (Jarjoura, 2013). This program offers a residential setting with on-site services such as employment, entrepreneurial programs, and job training in addition to mentoring and counseling.

The Mentoring Center (2018), located in Oakland, California, has trademarked its approach as "transformative mentoring." Primarily geared toward youth of color, the program uses a structured curriculum with a long-term group mentoring component. The curriculum rests on such foci as life skills training, stress and anger management, spiritual development, character development, career education and training, and cognitive restructuring (The Mentoring Center, 2018).

It is easy to understand how the principles of effective mentoring relationships mirror those of other therapeutic modes. Well-being springs from a sense of purpose and meaningful relationships, a hope for the future, and a sense of self-efficacy that gives a young male the belief that he can achieve his goals. Good mentoring relationships contribute to prosocial development in the cognitive, identity development, and socioemotional domains (Jarjoura, 2013).

Mentors for boys at-risk are advocates and conduits between school, home, and community on the boy's behalf, modeling the skills the young man can adopt in his own advocacy efforts. For too many boys, trauma-informed mentoring is essential, given that so many have been exposed to violence and have experienced trauma—both of which impede health and well-being (Youth Collaboratory, 2018). Perhaps the best setting possible to produce healthy masculinity is one that includes both counseling and mentoring, either in one-to-one or group settings.

FINAL THOUGHTS

There is a visible shift in theory and practice as it relates to counseling and therapy with boys and young men. As far back as the 1980s, there was important scholarly writing and research that discussed the mismatch between the most frequently used techniques and settings in traditional counseling and the needs and preferences of males. Since boys and adolescent males process and produce expressive language very differently from females, the models of talk therapy that have dominated professional practice for so long have proven ineffective and uncomfortable for most boys and men. Now, more than ever, new therapies and interventions are needed to address the problems of our male population.

There are benefits to framing counseling or therapy in male-friendly ways. These include using active or adventure-based models of therapy; forming all-male groups; framing therapy as a collective or collaborative effort in problem-solving; and taking therapy out of the office and into different locations that are more conducive to boys' action-orientation. Preventative interventions that target vulnerable groups before problems arise or escalate are also beneficial. Cracking the boy code before it does damage is far better than trying to undo damage in adult males.

Males rarely arrive at therapy sessions of their own volition or in a stage of change-orientation that suggests that readiness for working on problems. Nesting therapy into other formats, such as mentorships or group activities, makes it less likely that boys and young males will be avoidant. Describing therapeutic activities as work to be done, problems to be solved, rather than suggesting that something is wrong with the boy may entice boys into a deeper exploration of self, and motivational interviewing is one technique that may help uncover individual motivations to engage.

Some authors suggest that males should be defined as a marginalized group, like other culturally different subgroups. This then entails that counselors and therapists should be culturally competent or, in more recent terms, enter the relationship with cultural humility. They should be well-versed in the socialization processes that bring problematic attitudes and behaviors and threaten mental health and well-being in young males. Therapists who are ready to roll up their sleeves, work collaboratively, listen actively, use humor, appear as genuine individuals, and self-disclose when relevant and appropriate are most highly prized by boys.

So many young men and boys are in psychic pain and there often are few resources available to help them, particularly in impoverished and isolated areas. While schools find themselves in the unfortunate position of acting as mental health clinics for many students, it behooves us as a society to develop and offer a wide array of psychoeducational and therapeutic programs and whenever possible, to pair these with one-to-one counseling. Looking to programs that bolster mental health, resiliency, and well-being in the very young appears to be the route to healthier masculinity at all stages of the life span.

POINTS TO REMEMBER

- The institution of psychotherapy has been built by men but is not male friendly.
- Much more attention needs to be paid to health and wellness programs that are preventative in nature.
- Boys and young males prefer active, group-oriented, out-of-the-office modes of counseling.
- Men and boys rarely go to counseling of their own volition and with a readiness to seek change; therefore, first contacts with therapists and speaking in male terms with a knowledge of socialization patterns of boys and young men is crucial in order to form effective therapeutic alliances.
- Groups can be formed around particular attributes shared by the young males so that therapy can be delivered in the format that most prefer to include active, group supported, problem-solving methods.
- Men historically have been socialized to be storytellers, so the use of stories, myths, symbolism, and the like is a good place to hear males out, help them identify themes in their stories, and then attach emotional vocabulary to those themes.

References

American Psychological Association. (2019). *The changing role of the modern day father.* Retrieved from https://www.apa.org/pi/families/resources/changing-father

American School Counselors Association (2019). ASCA School Counselor Professional Standards & Competencies. Alexandria, VA: Author. Retrieved from https://www.schoolcounselor.org/asca/media/asca/home/SCCompetencies.pdf

Arnett, J. J. (2015). *Emerging adulthood: The winding road from the late tends through the twenties* (second ed.). New York, NY: Oxford University Press.

Baxter Magolda, M. B. (2008). Three elements of self-authorship. *Journal of College Student Development, 49*(4), 269–284. DOI: 10.1353/csd.0.0016

Benson, J. E., and Elder, G. H. (2011). Young adult identities and their pathways: A developmental and life course model. *Developmental Psychology, 47*(6), 1646–1657. DOI: 10.1037/a0023833

Bento, G., and Dias, G. (2017). The importance of outdoor play for young children's healthy development. *Porto Biomedical Journal, 2*(5), 157–160. DOI: 10.1016/j.pbj.2017.03003

Bergman, S. J. (1995). Men's psychological development: A relational perspective. In R. F. Levant and W. S. Pollack (Eds.), *A New Psychology of Men* (pp. 68–90). New York, NY: HarperCollins.

Berk, L. E. (2017). *Child Development.* Saddle River, NJ: Pearson Education.

Black, M. I. (2018). The boys are not all right. *The New York Times.* Retrieved from https://www.nytimes.com/2018/02/21/opinion/boys-violence-shootings-guns.html?module=inline

Bloom, D. (2016). *Instead of detention, these students get meditation.* Retrieved from https://www.cnn.com/2016/11/04/health/meditation-in-schools-baltimore/index.html

Borghans, L., Duckworth, A., Heckman, J., and Weel, B. ter. (2008). The economics and psychology of personality traits. *Journal of Human Resources, 43*(4), 972–1059.

Borrero, N. E., and Yeh, C. J. (2011). The multidimensionality of ethnic identity among urban high school youth. *Identity: An International Journal of Theory and Research, 11*(2), 114–135. DOI: 10.1080/15283488.2011.555978

Boyle, P. (2012). *What Scout abuse scandal teaches us.* Retrieved from https://www-m.cnn.com/2012/09/20/opinion/boyle-boy-scouts-abuse-scandal/index.html?r=https%3A%2F%2Fwww.google.com%2F

Bradshaw, C. P., Waasdorp, T. E., and Leaf, P. J. (2012). Effects of school-wide positive behavioral intervention and supports on child behavior problems. *Pediatrics, 130*(5), e1136–e1145. DOI: 10.1542/peds.2012-0243

Brooks, G. R. (1995). *The centerfold syndrome: How men can overcome objectification and achieve intimacy with women.* San Francisco, CA: Jossey-Bass.

Brooks, G. R. (1998). *A new psychotherapy for traditional men*. San Francisco, CA: Jossey-Bass.

Brooks, G. R. (2017). Counseling, psychotherapy, and psychological interventions for boys and men. In R. F. Levant and Y. J. Wong (Eds.), *The Psychology of Men and Masculinities* (pp. 317–345). Washington, D.C.: American Psychological Association.

Brown, C. M., and Smirles, K. E. (2003). Examining the bicultural ethnic identity of American Indian adolescents. *American Indian Culture and Research Journal, 29*(3), 81–100. Retrieved from http://www.books.aisc.ucla.edu/toc/aicrjv29n3.html

Brown, D. F., and Knowles, T. (2007). *What every middle school teacher should know* (third ed.). Portsmouth, NH: Heinemann.

Brown, V., and Olson, K. (2015). *The mindful school leader: Practices to transform your leadership and school*. Thousand Oaks, CA: Corwin: A Sage Company.

BRYCS. (2011). *Refugee children in US schools: A toolkit for teachers (Tool 4: Refugee and immigrant youth and bullying)*. Retrieved from https://brycs.org/toolkit/refugee-children-in-u-s-schools-a-toolkit-for-teachers-and-school-personnel/

Caldwell, L. D., and White, J. L. (2005). African-centered therapy and counseling interventions for African American males. In G. E. Good and G. R. Brooks (Eds.), *The New Handbook of Psychotherapy and Counseling with Men* (pp. 323–336). San Francisco, CA: Jossey-Bass.

Casas, J. M., Turner, J. A., and Ruiz de Esparza, C. A. (2005). Machismo revisited in a time of crisis: Implications for understanding and counseling Hispanic men. In G. E. Good and G. R. Brooks (Eds.), *The New Handbook of Psychotherapy and Counseling with Men* (pp. 337–356). San Francisco, CA: Jossey-Bass.

Cass, V. (1979). Homosexuality identity formation: A theoretical model. *Journal of Homosexuality, (4)*3, 219–235. DOI: 10.1300/J082v04n03_01

Cass, V. (1984). Homosexual identity formation: Testing a theoretical model. *The Journal of Sex Research* 20(2), 143–167. DOI: 10.1080/00224498409551214

CAST. (2019). *About universal design for learning*. Retrieved from http://www.cast.org/our-work/about-udl.html#.XFjm4lxKg2w

Castillo, L. G., Perez, F. V., Castillo, R., and Ghosheh, M. R. (2010). Construction and initial validation of the marianismo beliefs scale. *Counseling Psychology Quarterly, 23*(2), 163–175. DOI: 10.1080/09515071003776036

Chapin, L. (2015). Mexican-American boys' positive outcomes and resilience. *Journal of Child and Family Studies, 24*(6), 1791–1799. DOI: 10.1007/s10826-014-9982-8

Cherry, K. (2019). *Child development theories and examples*. Retrieved from https://www.verywellmind.com/child-development-theories-2795068

Chess, S., and Thomas, A. (1996). *Temperament: Theory and practice*. New York, NY: Brunner/Mazel.

Child Trends Databank. (2018). *High school dropout rates*. Retrieved from https://www.childtrends.org/indicators/high-school-dropout-rates

Chu, J. Y. (2014). *When boys become boys: Development, relationships, and masculinity*. New York, NY: New York University Press.

Collazo, R. (2016). *Why hypermasculinity is toxic for black men*. Retrieved from http://affinity-magazine.us/2016/05/22/why-hypermasculinity-is-toxic-for-black-men/

Cox, A. J. (2006). *Boys of few words: Raising our sons to communicate and connect*. New York, NY: Guilford Press

Cross, W. E. (1971). The Negro-to-Black conversion experience: Toward a psychology of Black liberation. *Black World, 20*(9), 13–27. Retrieved from https://eric.ed.gov/?id=EJ041879

Cross, W. E. (1991). *Shades of black: Diversity in African-American identity*. Philadelphia, PA: Temple University Press.

Cross, W. E., and Fhagen-Smith, P. (2001). Patterns of African American Identity Development: A Life Span Perspective. In C. L. Wijeyesinghe and B. W. Jackson, III (Eds.), *New Perspectives on Racial Identity Development: A Theoretical and Practical Anthology* (pp. 243–268). New York, NY: New York University Press.

Dancy, T. E. (2007). *Manhood constructions among engaged African American collegians: Influences, experiences, and contexts*. Retrieved from https://digitalcommons.lsu.edu/cgi/

viewcontent.cgi?referer=https://www.google.com/&httpsredir=1&article=3739&context =gradschool_dissertations

DeAngelis, T. (2014). Building resilience among black boys. *American Psychological Association, 45*(9), 50. Retrieved from https://www.apa.org/monitor/2014/10/cover-resilience

Derman-Sparks, L. (2012). *Stages in children's development of racial/cultural identity and attitudes.* Retrieved from https://www.uua.org/sites/live-new.uua.org/files/documents/dermansparkslouise/1206_233_identity_stages.pdf

Dhuey, E., Figlio, D., Karbownik, K., and Roth, J. (2017). School starting age and cognitive-development. *The National Bureau of Economic Research.* Retrieved from https://www.nber.org/papers/w23660

DiGioia, M. (2018). *Don't trust anyone over 30.* Retrieved from http://www.lumpenmagazine.org/dont-trust-anyone-over-30/

DiPrete, T. A., and Buchmann, C. (2013). *The rise of women: The growing gender gap in education and what it means for American schools.* New York, NY: Russell Sage Foundation.

Dobson, J. (2001). *Bringing up boys.* Carol Stream, IL: Tyndale Momentum.

Dowd, R. (2018). *Mental health of young adults with lesbian parents the same as their peers, study finds.* Retrieved from https://williamsinstitute.law.ucla.edu/press/nllfs-young-adults-press-release/

Dwedar, M. (2016). "Like walking into a hailstorm": Discrimination against LGBT youth in United States schools. Human Rights Watch. Retrieved from https://www.hrw.org/sites/default/files/report_pdf/uslgbt1216web_2.pdf

Early Childhood National Centers & the National Center on Parent, Family, and Community Engagement. (n.d.). *Healthy gender development and young children: A guide for early childhood programs and professionals.* Retrieved from https://eclkc.ohs.acf.hhs.gov/sites/default/files/pdf/healthy-gender-development.pdf

Ebert, M., and Flynn, L. (2014). *An antidote to teacher burnout: How yoga and mindfulness can support resilience in and out of the classroom.* Retrieved from http://www.yoga4classrooms.com/yoga-4-classrooms-blog/Teacher-Burnout-yoga-mindfulness-for-teacher-resilience-classroom

Eichenfield, G. A. (1996). University-based group therapy for faculty, students, and staff. In M. P. Andronico, *Men in Groups: Insights, Interviews, Psychoeducational work* (pp. 81–96). Washington, DC: American Psychological Association. DOI: 10.1037/10284-000

Eichhorn, D. H. (1968). *Planning programs for transescents.* Retrieved from https://files.eric.ed.gov/fulltext/ED033445.pdf

Elium, D., and Elium, J. (2004). *Raising a son* (third ed.). New York, NY: Random House.

Englar-Carlson, M., Evans, M. P., and Duffey, T. (2014). *A counselor's guide to working with men.* Retrieved from https://www.counseling.org/Publications/FrontMatter/78086-FM.PDF

Epstein, J. (2010). *School, family, and community partnerships: Preparing educators and empowering schools.* Boulder, CO: Westview Press.

Erickson, B. (1993). *Helping men change: The role of the female therapist.* Thousand Oaks, CA: Sage.

Erikson, E. (1980). *Identity and the life cycle.* New York, NY: W.W. Norton & Company.

Erickson, J. J. (2018). *Rediscovering the indispensable role of fathers.* Retrieved from https://www.deseretnews.com/article/900021781/the-indispensable-role-of-fathers.html

Evans, L., and Davies, K. (2000). No sissy boys here: A content analysis of the representation of masculinity in elementary school reading textbooks. *Sex Roles 42*(3/4), 255–270. DOI: 10.1023/A:1007043323906

Fassinger, R. E., and Miller, B. A. (1996). Validation of an inclusive model of homosexual identity formation in a sample of gay men. *Journal of Homosexuality, 32*(2), 53–78. DOI: 10.1300/J082v32n02_04

Fazel, M., Hoagwood, K., Stephan, S., and Ford, T. (2014). Mental health interventions in schools 1: Mental health interventions in schools in high-income countries. *The lancet. Psychiatry, 1*(5), 377–387. DOI: 10.1016/S2215-0366(14)70312-8

Ferdman, B. M., and Gallegos, P. I. (2001). Latinos and racial identity development. In C. L. Wijeyesinghe and B. W. Jackson III (Eds.), *New perspectives on racial identity develop-*

ment: A theoretical and practical anthology (pp. 32–66). New York, NY: New York University Press.

Firestone, L. (2012). *7 tips to raising an emotionally healthy child.* Retrieved from https://www.psychologytoday.com/us/blog/compassion-matters/201211/7-tips-raising-emotionally-healthy-child

Fleming, M. C., and Englar-Carlson, M. (2008). Examining depression and suicidality in boys and male adolescents. In M. S. Kiselica, M. Englar-Carlson, and A. M. Horne (Eds.), *Counseling Troubled Boys: A Guidebook for Professionals* (pp. 125–161). New York, NY: Taylor & Francis.

Garrett, M. T. (1996). "Two people": An American Indian narrative of bicultural identity. *Journal of American Indian Education, 36*(1), 1–21. Retrieved from https://www.jstor.org/stable/24398477

Garringer, M. (2004). *Putting the "men" back in mentoring.* Retrieved from https://education-northwest.org/sites/default/files/resources/bulletin_male_recruitment.pdf

Gay, G. (1994). Coming of age ethically: Teaching young adolescents of color. *Theory into Practice, 33*(3), 149–155. DOI: 10.1080/00405849409543633

Ghosh, S. (2015). *Gender Identity.* Retrieved from https://emedicine.medscape.com/article/917990-overview

Gilpin, C. C., and Proulx, N. (2018). *Boys to men: Teaching and learning about masculinity in an age of change.* Retrieved from https://www.nytimes.com/2018/04/12/learning/lesson-plans/boys-to-men-teaching-and-learning-about-masculinity-in-an-age-of-change.html

Goleman, D. (2006). *Social intelligence: The new science of human relationships.* New York, NY: Random House.

Gonzales, K. G. (2016). *Counseling groups for at-risk minority male adolescents* (Unpublished dissertation). Rutgers University, NJ. Retrieved from https://rucore.libraries.rutgers.edu/rutgers-lib/49841/PDF/1/play/

Goulding, M. M., and Goulding, R. L. (1997). *Changing lives through redecision therapy.* New York, NY: Grove Press.

Gove, A., and Cvelich, P. (2011). *Early reading: Igniting education for all. A report by the early grade learning community of practice.* Retrieved from https://eric.ed.gov/?id=ED520290

Greer, M. (2005). Keeping 'em hooked. *Monitor on Psychology, 36*(7), 60–63. Retrieved from https://www.apa.org/monitor/jun05/hooked

Grover, S. (2016). *Boys without fathers: 3 myths, 3 miracles.* Retrieved from https://www.psychologytoday.com/us/blog/when-kids-call-the-shots/201606/boys-without-fathers-3-myths-3-miracles

Gruber, J., and Borelli, J. L. (2017). *The importance of fostering emotional diversity in boys.* Retrieved from https://www.scientificamerican.com/article/the-importance-of-fostering-emotional-diversity-in-boys/

Guo, J. (2016). The serious reason boys do worse than girls. *The Washington Post.* Retrieved from https://www.washingtonpost.com/news/wonk/wp/2016/01/28/the-serious-reason-boys-do-worse-than-girls/?noredirect=on&utm_term=.642154fdd995

Gurian, M. (1997). *The wonder of boys.* New York, NY: Penguin Putnam.

Gurian, M. (1999). 10 things each of us can do to help our adolescent boys. Retrieved from https://sparkaction.org/content/10-things-each-us-can-do-help-our-adolescent-boys

Gurian, M. (2001). *Boys and girls learn differently! A guide for teachers and parents.* San Francisco, CA: Jossey-Bass.

Haines, E. L., Deaux, K., and Lofaro, N. (2016). The times they are a-changing . . . or are they not? A comparison of gender stereotypes, 1938–2014. *Psychology of Women Quarterly, 40*(3), 353–363. DOI: 10.1177/0361684316634081

Halderman, D. C. (2005). Psychotherapy with gay and bisexual men. In R. Levant and W. Pollack (Eds.), *A New Psychology of Men* (pp. 369–383). New York, NY: Basic Books.

Hall, A. (2017). *Study finds just how differently moms & dads parent their kids, & the reasons probably won't surprise you.* Retrieved from https://www.romper.com/p/study-finds-just-how-differently-moms-dads-parent-their-kids-the-reasons-probably-wont-surprise-you-6765814

Harvard University. (2015). The importance of recess. *Harvard Health Publishing.* Retrieved from https://www.health.harvard.edu/exercise-and-fitness/the-importance-of-recess

Hattori, K. (2014). *Four steps to cultivating compassion in boys.* Retrieved from https://greater-good.berkeley.edu/article/item/four_steps_to_cultivating_compassion_in_boys

Havighurst, R. J. (1963). *Adolescent characteristics and personality.* New York, NY: Science Editions.

Herring, R. (1999). Helping Native American Indian and Alaska Native youth. In A. M. Horne and M. S. Kiselica (Eds.), *Handbook of counseling boys and adolescent males* (pp. 117–136). Thousand Oaks, CA: Sage.

Heyder, A., and Kessels, U. (2013). Is school feminine? Implicit gender stereotyping of school as a predictor of academic achievement. *Sex Roles, 69*(11–12), 605–617. DOI: 10.1007/s11199-013-0309-9

Higgins, E. T. (1987). Self-Discrepancy: a theory relating self and affect. *Psychological Review , 94*(3), 319–340. DOI: 10.1037/0033-295X.94.3.319

Hill, J. P., and Lynch, M. E. (1983). The intensification of gender-related role expectations during early adolescence. In J. Brooks-Gunn and A. C. Petersen (Eds.), *Girls at puberty* (pp. 201–228). New York, NY: Springer.

Holcomb-McCoy, C. (2005). Ethnic identity development in early adolescence: Implications and recommendations for middle school counselors. *Professional School Counseling, 9*(2), 120–127. DOI: 10.1177/2156759X0500900204

Hook, N., Davis, D., Owen, J., and DeBlaere, C. (2017). *Cultural Humility: Engaging Diverse Identities in Therapy.* Washington, DC: American Psychological Association.

Horne, A. M., Jolliff, D., and Roth, E. (1996). Men mentoring men in groups. In M. Andronica (Ed.), *Men in Groups: Insight, Interventions, Psychoeducational Work* (pp. 97–112). Washington, DC: American Psychological Association.

Horne, A. M., and Kiselica, M. S. (1999). *Handbook of counseling boys and adolescent males: A practitioner's guide.* Thousand Oaks, CA: Sage.

Horse, P. G. (2005). Native American identity. *New Directions for Student Services, 109,* 61–68. DOI: 10.1002/ss.154

Hoyt, D. (2015). *Understanding the minds of boys: Strategies for student engagement.* Retrieved from http://inservice.ascd.org/understanding-the-minds-of-boys-strategies-for-student-engagement/

Jackson, C., and Dempster, S. (2009). "I sat back on my computer . . . with a bottle of whisky next to me": Constructing "cool" masculinity through "effortless" achievement in secondary and higher education. *Journal of Gender Studies, 18*(4), 341–356. DOI: 10.1080/09589230903260019

Jarjoura, G. R. (2013). Effective strategies for mentoring African American boys. Retrieved from https://www.air.org/sites/default/files/downloads/report/Effective%20Strategies%20for%20Mentoring%20African%20American%20Boys.pdf

Jean, E., and Buckley, D. L. (2019). Gender and sexual orientation: Understanding the differences among students. In N. D. Young, E. Jean (Bienia), and T. A. Citro. (2019). *Acceptance, understanding, and the moral imperative of promoting social justice education in the schoolhouse* (pp. 37–48). Wilmington, DE: Vernon Press.

Jean, E., and Rotas, G. (2019). Fostering growth in the classroom: Climate, culture, and supports that make a difference. In N. D. Young, E. Jean, and C. N. Michaels, *Empathic Teaching: Promoting social justice in the contemporary classroom,* pp. 13–30. Wilmington, DE: Vernon Press.

Jensen, E. (2009). *Teaching with poverty in mind: What being poor does to kids' brains and what schools can do about it.* Alexandria, VA: ASCD.

Jensen, F. E., and Nutt, A. (2015). *The teenage brain: A neuroscientist's survival guide to raising adolescents and young males.* New York, NY: Harper Paperbacks.

Jewkes, R., Morrell, R., Hearn, J., Lundqvist, E., Blackbeard, D., Lindegger, G., and Gottzen, L. (2015). Hegemonic masculinity: Combining theory and practice in gender interventions. *Culture, Health & Sexuality, 17*(2), S112–S127. DOI: 10.1080/13691058.2015.1084094

Jha, J., and Pouezevara, S. (2016). *Measurement and research support to education strategy goal 1: Boys' underachievement in education: A review of the literature with a focus on reading in the early years.* Retrieved from http://www.ungei.org/Boys_Underachievement. pdf

Johnson, N. G. (2005). Women helping men: Strengths of and barriers to women therapists working with men clients. In G. R. Brooks and G. E. Good (Eds.), *The New Handbook of Psychotherapy and Counseling with Men* (vol. 2) (pp. 291–307). San Francisco, CA: Jossey Bass.

Jolliff, D., and Horne, A. M. (1999). Growing up male: The development of mature masculinity. In Horne, A. M. and Kiselica, M. S. (1999). *Handbook of Counseling Boys and Adolescent Males* (pp. 3–24). Thousand Oaks, CA: Sage.

Kabat-Zinn, J. (2005). *Wherever you go, there you are: Mindfulness meditation in everyday life.* Boston, MA: Hachette Books.

Kastner, L. (2018). *How boys suffer: The boy code and toxic masculinity.* Retrieved from https://www.parentmap.com/article/how-boys-suffer-the-boy-code-and-toxic-masculinity

Katz-Wise, S. L., Budge, S., Fugate, E., Flanagan, K., Touloumtzis, C., Rood, B., and Lebowitz, S. (2017). Transactional pathways of transgender identity development in transgender and gender nonconforming youth and caregivers from the trans youth family study. *International Journal of Transgenderism, 18*(3), 243–263. DOI: 10.1080/15532739.2017.1304312

Keltner, D. (2018). *Hands on research: The science of touch.* Retrieved from https://greatergood.berkeley.edu/article/item/hands_on_research/

Kim J. (1981). *The processes of Asian American identity development: A study of Japanese American women's perceptions of their struggle to achieve positive identities as Americans of Asian ancestry.* Retrieved from https://scholarworks.umass.edu/cgi/viewcontent.cgi?referer=https://www.google.com/&httpsredir=1&article=4686&context=dissertations_1

Kindlon, D., and Thompson, M. (2000). *Raising Cain: Protecting the emotional life of boys.* New York, NY: Random House.

King, L. A., and King, D. W. (1993). *SRES: Sex-role egalitarianism scale.* Retrieved from https://www.sigmaassessmentsystems.com/assessments/sex-role-egalitarianism-scale/

Kiselica, M. S. (2005). A male-friendly therapeutic process with school-age boys. In G. E. Good and G. R. Brooks (Eds.), *The New Handbook of Psychotherapy and Counseling with Men* (pp. 17–28). San Francisco, CA: Jossey-Bass.

Kiselica, M. S., Englar-Carlson, M., Horne, A. M., and Fisher, M. (2008). A positive psychology perspective on helping boys. In M. S. Kiselica, M. Englar-Carlson, and A. M. Horne (Eds), *Counseling Troubled Boys: A Guidebook for Professionals* (pp. 31–48). New York, NY: Taylor & Francis.

Knight, D. J. (2015). *Beyond the stereotypical image of young men of color.* Retrieved from https://www.theatlantic.com/education/archive/2015/01/beyond-the-stereotypical-image-of-young-men-of-color/384194/

Konik, J., and Stewart, A. (2004). Sexual identity development in the context of compulsory heterosexuality. *Journal of Personality, 72*(4), 815-844. DOI: 10.1111/j.0022-3506.2004.00281.x

Kosciw, J. G., Greytak, E. A., Giga, N. M., Vilenas, C., and Danischeswski, D. J. (2015). *The 2015 national school climate survey: The experience of lesbian, gay, bisexual, transgender, and queer youth in our nation's schools.* Retrieved from https://www.glsen.org/sites/default/files/2015%20National%20GLSEN%202015%20National%20School%20Climate%20Survey%20%28NSCS%29%20-%20Full%20Report_0.pdf

Kroger, J. (2007). *Identity development: Adolescence through adulthood.* Thousand Oaks, CA: Sage.

Krugman S. (1995). Male development and the transformation of shame. In R. F. Levant and W. S. Pollack (Eds.), *A New Psychology of Men* (pp. 91–126). New York, NY: Basic Books.

Kuper, S., and Jacobs, E. (2019). *The untold danger of boys falling behind in school.* Retrieved from https://www.ozy.com/fast-forward/why-are-boys-falling-behind-in-school/91361

Lahey, J. (2013). *Stop penalizing boys for not being able to sit still at school.* Retrieved from https://www.theatlantic.com/sexes/archive/2013/06/stop-penalizing-boys-for-not-being-able-to-sit-still-at-school/276976/

Lamb, M. E. (1995). The changing roles of fathers. In J. L. Shapiro, M. J. Diamond, and M. Greenberg (Eds.), Springer series, focus on men, Vol. 8. Becoming a father: Contemporary, social, developmental, and clinical perspectives (pp. 18–35). New York, NY: Springer Publishing Co. (Reprinted in modified form from M. Lamb (Ed.), "The Father's Role: Applied Perspectives," New York, NY: Wiley, 1986, pp. 3–27.)

Lang, N. (2018). *New study: Rates of anti-LGBTQ school bullying at "unprecedented High."* Retrieved from https://www.thedailybeast.com/new-study-rates-of-anti-lgbtq-school-bullying-at-unprecedented-high

Lassiter, C. J. (2017). *The 4 types of everyday courage.* Retrieved from http://corwin-connect.com/2017/01/4-types-everyday-courage/

Lee, C. (2008). The centrality of culture to the scientific study of learning and development: How an ecological framework in education research facilitates civic responsibility. *Educational Researcher, 37,* 267–279. DOI: 10.3102/0013189X08322683

Levant, R. F. (1995). Toward the reconstruction of masculinity. In R. Levant and W. Pollack (Eds.), *A New Psychology of Men* (pp. 229–251). New York, NY: Basic Books.

Levant, R. F. (2005). The crises of boyhood. In G. E. Good and G. R. Brooks (Eds.), *The New Handbook of Psychotherapy and Counseling with Men* (pp. 161–171). San Francisco, CA: Jossey-Bass.

Levant, R., and Pollack, W. (2005). *A New Psychology of Men.* New York, NY: Basic Books.

Levinson, D. J. (1978). *The seasons of a man's life.* New York, NY: Ballantine.

Levy, D. L. (2009). Gay and lesbian identity development: An overview for social workers. *Journal of Human Behavior in the Social Environment, 19*(8), 978–993. DOI: 10.1080/10911350903126866

Liu, L. (2016). Study reveals LGBT students face unprecedented violence in high schools nationwide. Retrieved from http://www.businessinsider.com/lgbt-high-school-students-face-violence-nationwide-2016-8

Liu, W. M., Shepard, S. J., and Nicpon, M. F. (2008). "Boys are tough, not smart": Counseling gifted and talented young and adolescent boys. In M. S. Kiselica, M. Englar-Carlson, and A. M. Horne (Eds), *Counseling Troubled Boys: A Guidebook for Professionals* (pp. 273–291). New York, NY: Taylor & Francis.

López, E. J., Ehly, S., and Garcia-Vazquez, E. (2002). Acculturation, social support and academic achievement of Mexican and Mexican American high school students: An exploratory study. *Psychology in the Schools, 39*(3), 245–257. DOI: 10.1002/pits.10009

Mahalik, J. R. (1999). Incorporating a gender role strain perspective in assessing and treating Men's cognitive distortions. *Professional Psychology: Research and Practice, 30*(4), 333–340. DOI: 10.1037/0735-7028.30.4.333

Mahler, M. S., Pine, F., and Bergman, A. (2000). *The psychological birth of the human infant.* New York, NY: Basic Books.

Maples, M. R., and Robertson, J. M. (2005). Counseling men with religious affiliations. In G. R. Brooks and G. E. Good (Eds.), *The New Handbook of Psychotherapy and Counseling with Men* (vol. 2) (pp. 816–843). San Francisco, CA: Jossey Bass.

Marcia, J. E. (1966). Development and validation of ego identity status. *Journal of Personality and Social Psychology, 3*(5), 551–558. DOI: 10.1037/h0023281

Marcia, J. E. (1980). Identity in adolescence. In J. Adelson (Ed.), *Handbook of Adolescent Psychology* (pp. 159–187). San Francisco, CA: Wiley.

Marcoux, H. (2018). *Major long-term study: Kids with lesbian parents grow up to be happy adults.* Retrieved from https://www.mother.ly/news/lesbian-parents-impact-kids-mental-health

Marks, J., Bun, L. C., and McHale, S. M. (2009). Family patterns of gender role attitudes. *Sex Roles, 61*(3–4), 221–234. DOI: 10.1007/s11199-009-9619-3

Markus, H., and Nurius, P. (1986). Possible selves. *American Psychologist, 41,* 954–969. DOI: 10.1037/0003-066X.41.9.954

Matthews, J. S., Banerjee, M., and Lauerman, F. (2014). Academic Identity Formation and Motivation Among Ethnic Minority Adolescents: The Role of the "Self" Between Internal and External Perceptions of Identity. *Child Development, 85*(6), 2355–2373. DOI: 10.1111/cdev.12318

Maynard, B. R., Vaughn, M. G., Salas-Wright, C. P., and Vaughn, S. R. (2016). Bullying victimization among school-aged immigrant youth in the United States. *Journal of Adolescent Health, 58*(3), 337–344. DOI: 10.1016/j.adohealth.2015.11.013

McFarland, J., Hussar, B., Wang, X., Zhang, J., Wang, K., Rathbun, A., and Bullock Mann, F. (2018). *The condition of education 2018.* Washington, DC: National Center for Education Statistics. U.S. Department of Education. Retrieved from https://nces.ed.gov/pubs2018/2018144.pdf

McGeown, S., Goodwin, H., Henderson, N., and Wright, P. (2012). Gender differences in reading motivation: Does sex or gender identity provide a better account? *Journal of Research in Reading, 35*(3), 328–336. DOI: 10.1111/j.1467-9817.2010.01481.x

McKay, T., Lindquist, C. H., and Misra, S. (2017). Understanding (and acting on) 20 years of research on violence and LGBTQ+ communities. *Trauma, Violence, & Abuse.* DOI: 10.1177/1524838017728708

Miller, C. (2016). *Building champions: A small-group counseling curriculum for boys.* Champaign, IL: Research Press Publishers.

Mindful Schools. (2019). *Why mindfulness is needed in education: The impact of toxic stress on school communities.* Retrieved from https://www.mindfulschools.org/about-mindfulness/mindfulness-in-education/

Ministry of Education. (2009). *Me read? And how! Ontario teachers report on how to improve boys' literacy skills.* Retrieved from http://www.edu.gov.on.ca/eng/curriculum/meread_andhow.pdf

Moon, P. (2018). *Operation: Breaking the Boy Code.* Chapin, SC: Youth Light Inc.

Murray, D. W., and Rosanbalm, K. (2017). *Promoting Self-Regulation in Adolescents and Young Adults: A Practice Brief.* OPRE Report #2015–82. Washington, DC: Office of Planning, Research, and Evaluation, Administration for Children and Families, U.S. Department of Health and Human Services. Retrieved from https://www.acf.hhs.gov/sites/default/files/opre/sr_ado_brief_revised_2_15_2017_508.pdf

Musu-Gillette, L., de Brey, C., McFarland, J., Hussar, W., Sonnenberg, W., and Wilkinson-Flicker, S. (2017). *Status and trends in the education of racial and ethnic groups 2017.* U.S. Department of Education, National Center for Education Statistics. Retrieved from https://nces.ed.gov/pubs2017/2017051.pdf

My Brother's Keeper Alliance and MENTOR: The National Mentoring Partnership. (2016). *Guide to mentoring boys and young men of color.* Retrieved from https://www.mentoring.org/new-site/wp-content/uploads/2016/05/Guide-to-Mentoring-BYMOC.pdf

National Resource Center for Mental Health Promotion and Youth Violence Prevention, (n.d.). *Adopting a trauma-informed approach for LGBTQ youth: A two-part resource for schools and agencies: Why use a trauma-informed approach with LGBTQ youth?* Retrieved from https://healthysafechildren.org/sites/default/files/Trauma_Informed_Approach_LGBTQ_Youth_1.pdf

National Scientific Council on the Developing Child. (2014). Excessive Stress Disrupts the Architecture of the Developing Brain: Working Paper 3. Updated Edition. Retrieved from https://developingchild.harvard.edu/wp-content/uploads/2005/05/Stress_Disrupts_Architecture_Developing_Brain-1.pdf

Newkirk, T. (2002). *Misreading masculinity: boys, literacy, and pop culture.* Portsmouth, NH: Heinemann.

Nilsen, W., Karevold, E. B., Kaasbøll, J., and Kjeldsen, A. (2018). Nuancing the role of social skills—a longitudinal study of early maternal psychological distress and adolescent depressive symptoms. *BMC Pediatrics, 18*(1), 133. DOI: 10.1186/s12887-018-1100-4

Noguera, P. A. (2008). *The trouble with Black boys . . . and other reflections on race, equity, and the future of public education.* San Francisco, CA: Wiley & Sons.

Northwestern University. (2008, March 5). Boys' and Girls' Brains Are Different: Gender Differences in Language Appear Biological. *ScienceDaily.* Retrieved from www.sciencedaily.com/releases/2008/03/080303120346.htm

Olsen, J. (2017). *Many boys struggle with maintaining close friendships with one another during adolescence.* Retrieved from https://www.canr.msu.edu/news/many_boys_struggle_with_maintaining_close_friendships_with_one_another_duri

O'Neil, J. M. (2015). *Men's gender role conflict: Psychological costs, consequences, and an agenda for change.* Washington, DC: American Psychological Association.

O'Neil, J. M., Challenger, C., Renzulli, S., Crasper, B., and Webster, E. (2013). The Boy's Forum: An evaluation of a brief intervention to empower middle-school urban boys. *The Journal of Men's Studies, 27*(2), 191–205. DOI: 10.3149/jms.2102.191

O'Neil, J. M., and Egan, J. (1992). Men's and women's gender role journeys: A metaphor for healing, transition, and transformation. In B. R. Wainrib (Ed.), *Gender issues across the life cycle* (pp. 107–123). New York, NY: Springer Publishing Co.

Ortner, N. (2013). *The tapping solution: A revolutionary system for stress-free living.* New York, NY: Hay House.

Osborne, J. W., and Jones, B. D. (2011). Identification with Academics and Motivation to Achieve in School: How the Structure of the Self Influences Academic Outcomes. *Educational Psychology Review 23*(1), 131–158. DOI: 10.1007/s10648-011-9151-1

Osherson, S. (1986). *Finding our fathers: The unfinished business of manhood.* New York, NY: Free Press.

Oxford Dictionaries. (2019). *Teleology.* Retrieved from https://en.oxforddictionaries.com/definition/teleology

Oyserman, D., Bybee, D., Terry, K., and Hart-Johnson, T. (2004). Possible selves as Roadmaps. *Journal of Research in Personality , 38*(2), 130–149. DOI: 10.1016/S0092-6566(03)00057-6

Parker, K., and Stepler, R. (2017). Americans see men as the financial providers, even as women's contributions grow. *Pew Research Center.* Retrieved from https://www.pewresearch.org/fact-tank/2017/09/20/americans-see-men-as-the-financial-providers-even-as-womens-contributions-grow/

PBS Parents. (n.d.). *The Search for Masculinity: Understanding & raising boys: Growing up masculine.* Retrieved from http://www.pbs.org/parents/raisingboys/masculinity02.html

Perez-Gualdron, L., Yeh, C., and Russell, L. (2016). *Boys II Men: A culturally-responsive school counseling group for urban high school boys of color.* Retrieved from https://files.eric.ed.gov/fulltext/EJ1126013.pdf

Philpot, C. L., Brooks, G. R., Lusterman, D.-D., and Nutt, R. L. (1997). Bridging separate gender worlds: Why men and women clash and how therapists can bring them together. Washington, DC: American Psychological Association. DOI: 10.1037/10263-000

Phinney, J. S. (1993). A three-stage model of ethnic identity development in adolescence. In M. E. Bernal and G. P. Knight (Eds.), *Ethnic identity: Formation and transmission among Hispanics and other minorities* (pp. 61–79). New York, NY: State University of New York Press.

Phinney, J. S. (2003). Ethnic identity and acculturation. In K. M. Chun, P. Balls Organista, and G. Marin (Eds.), *Acculturation: Advances in theory, measurement, and applied research* (pp. 63–81). Washington, DC: American Psychological Association.

Phinney, J. S., and Ong, A. D. (2007). Conceptualization and Measurement of Ethnic Identity: Current Status and Future Directions. *Journal of Counseling Psychology, 54*(3), 271– 281. DOI; 10.1037/0022-0167.54.3.271

Pittman, F. (1993). *Man enough: Fathers, sons, and the search for masculinity.* New York, NY: Pedigree.

Pleck, J. H. (1995). The gender role strain paradigm: An update. In R. Levant and W. Pollack (Eds.), *A New Psychology of Men* (pp. 11–32). New York, NY: Basic Books.

Pollack, W. S. (1995). No man is an island: Toward a new psychoanalytic psychology of men. In R. Levant and W. Pollack (Eds.), *A New Psychology of Men* (pp. 33–67). New York, NY: Basic Books.

Pollack, W. S. (1998). *Real boys: Rescuing our sons from the myths of boyhood.* New York, NY: Henry Holt and Company.

Pollack, W. S. (2001). *Real boys' voices.* New York, NY: Penguin Books.

Pollack, W. S. (2005). "Masked men": New psychoanalytically oriented treatment models for adult and young adult men. In G. E. Good and G. R. Brooks (Eds.), *The New Handbook of Psychotherapy and Counseling with Men* (pp. 203–216). San Francisco, CA: Jossey-Bass.

Portrie-Bethke, T. L., Christian, D., Brown, W., and Hill, N. R. (2012). Navigating the challenges of connecting with male youth: Empowering real-time interventions through adventure-based counseling. In S. Degges-White and B. Colon (Eds.), *Counseling Boys and Young Men* (pp. 185–220). New York, NY: Springer Publishing Company.

Positive Behavioral Interventions and Supports. (2019a). *Classroom PBIS practices.* Retrieved from https://www.pbis.org/school/pbis-in-the-classroom/classroom-pbis-practices

Positive Behavioral Interventions and Supports. (2019b). *PBIS and the law.* Retrieved from https://www.pbis.org/school/pbis-and-the-law

Price, M. (2017). *Study finds some significant difference in brains of men and women.* Retrieved from https://www.sciencemag.org/news/2017/04/study-finds-some-significant-diff erences-brains-men-and-women

Prochaska, J. O., and DiClemente, C. C. (1982). Transtheoretical therapy: Toward a more integrative model of change. *Psychotherapy: Theory, Research & Practice, 19*(3), 276–288. DOI: 10.1037/h0088437

Rabinowitz, F. E. (2005). Group therapy for men. In G. E. Good and G. R. Brooks (Eds.), *The New Handbook of Psychotherapy and Counseling with Men* (pp. 264–277). San Francisco, CA: Jossey-Bass.

Rabinowitz, F. E. (2014). Counseling men in groups. In M. Englar-Carlson, M. P. Evans, and T. Duffey. *A counselor's guide to working with men* (pp. 55–70). Retrieved from https://www.counseling.org/Publications/FrontMatter/78086-FM.PDF

Raeburn, P. (2014). *Do fathers matter? What science is telling us about the parent we've overlooked.* New York, NY: Scientific American/Farrar, Straus and Giroux.

Reichert, M., and Hawley, R. (2010). *Reaching boys, teaching boys: Strategies that work—and why.* San Francisco, CA: John Wiley & Sons.

Reist, M. (2015). *Raising emotionally healthy boys.* Toronto, CAN: Dundurn.

Rice, R. P., and Dolgan, K. G. (2005). *The adolescent: Development, relationships, and culture.* Boston, MA: Pearson.

Rich, J. D. (2018). *Strict gender roles hurt men, too.* Retrieved from https://www.psychologytoday.com/us/blog/parenting-purpose/201803/strict-gender-roles-hurt-men-too-0

Ricks, D. (n.d.). Educating boys for success: Are today's classrooms biased against boys? *National Education Association.* Retrieved from http://www.nea.org/home/44609.htm

Rittenmeyer, L. (2002). *Moments in the hero journey of adolescent boys: A phenomenological inquiry into the lived experience of high school.* Doctoral dissertation: The Adler School of Professional Psychology.

Robert Wood Johnson Foundation. (2012). *Can tag help schools teach?* Retrieved from https://files.eric.ed.gov/fulltext/ED541164.pdf

Robertson, J. M., and Shepard, D. S. (2008). The psychological development of boys. In M. S. Kiselica, M. Englar-Carlson, and A. M. Horne (Eds.), *Counseling Troubled Boys: A Guidebook for Professionals* (pp. 3–29). New York, NY: Taylor & Francis.

Rogers, L. O., Scott, M. A., and Way, N. (2014). Racial and gender identity among Black adolescent males: An intersectionality perspective. *Child Development, 86*(2), 407–424. DOI: 10.1111/cdev.12303

Romero, A. J., and Roberts, R. E. (2003). Stress within a bicultural context for adolescents of mexican descent. *Cultural Diversity and Ethnic Minority Psychology, 9*(2), 171–184. DOI: 10.1037/1099-9809.9.2.171

Samuels, C. A. (2017). Delaying child's starting age for school a tough call for parents. *Education Week.* Retrieved from https://www.edweek.org/ew/articles/2017/08/30/delaying-childs-starting-age-for-school-a.html

Sanchez, D. T., Chaney, K. E., Manuel, S. K., and Remedios, J. D. (2018). Theory of prejudice and American identity threat transfer for Latino and Asian Americans. *Personality and Social Psychology Bulletin, 44*(7), 972–983. DOI: 10.1177/0146167218759288

Sankaran, S., Sekerdej, M., and von Hecker, U. (2017). The role of Indian caste identity and caste inconsistent norms on status representation. *Frontiers in Psychology, 8*(487), 1–14. DOI: 10.3389/fpsyg.2017.00487

Santos, C. E., Galligan, K., Pahlke, E., and Fabes, R. (2011). Gender-typed behaviors, achievement, and adjustment among racially and ethnically-diverse boys during early adolescence. *Journal of Orthopsychiatry , 83*(2PT3), 252–264. DOI: 10.1111/ajop.12036

Schneiderman, N., Ironson, G., and Siegel, S. D. (2005). Stress and health: psychological, behavioral, and biological determinants. *Annual Review of Clinical Psychology, 1*, 607–628. DOI: 10.1146/annurev.clinpsy.1.102803.144141

Scholz, R., and Hall, S. R. (2014). Motivational interviewing and masculine-sensitive therapy. In M. Englar-Carlson, M. P. Evans, and T. Duffey. *A counselor's guide to working with men* (pp. 325–346). Retrieved from https://www.counseling.org/Publications/FrontMatter/78086-FM.PDF

Schott Foundation for Public Education. (2015). *Black lives matter: The Schott 50 state report of public education and black males.* Retrieved from http://schottfoundation.org/resources/black-lives-matter-schott-50-state-report-public-education-and-black-males

Schwartz, S. J., and Petrova, M. (2018). Fostering healthy identity development in adolescence. *Nature Human Behavior, 2*(2), 110–111. DOI: 10.1038/s41562-017-0283-2

Seidler, Z. E., Rice, S. M., Ogrodniczuk, J. S., Oliffe, J. L., and Dhillon, H. M. (2018). Engaging Men in Psychological Treatment: A Scoping Review. *American Journal of Men's Health, 12*(6), 1882–1900. DOI: 10.1177/1557988318792157

Sheehy, G. (1986). *The victorious personality.* Retrieved from https://www.nytimes.com/1986/04/20/magazine/the-victorious-personality.html

Slocumb, P. D. (2007). *Hear our cry: Boys in crisis.* Highlands, TX: Aha! Process Inc.

Sommers, C. H. (2013a). How to make school better for boys. *The Atlantic.* Retrieved from https://www.theatlantic.com/education/archive/2013/09/how-to-make-school-better-for-boys/279635/

Sommers, C. H. (2013b). *The war against boys: How misguided policies are harming our young men.* New York, NY: Simon and Schuster.

Spielberg, W. (1999). A cultural critique of current practices of male adolescent identity formation. In A. M. Horne and M. S. Kiselica (Eds.), *Handbook of counseling boys and adolescent males* (pp. 25–34). Thousand Oaks, CA: Sage.

Spurgeon, S. L., and Paredes, D. M. (2012). Understanding male adolescent diversity. In S. Degges-White and B. Colon (Eds.), *Counseling Boys and Young Men* (pp. 41–57). New York: NY: Springer Publishing Company.

Su, R., Rounds, J., and Armstrong, P. L. (2009). Men and things, women and people: A meta-analysis of sex difference in interests. *Psychological Bulletin, 135*(6), 859–884. DOI: 10.1037/a0017364

Sue, D. W. (2010). *Microaggressions: More than just race.* Retrieved from https://www.psychologytoday.com/us/blog/microaggressions-in-everyday-life/201011/microaggressions-more-just-race

Sue, D. W., Sue, D., Neville, H. A., and Smith L. (2012). *Counseling the culturally diverse.* New York, NY: John Wiley & Sons.

Sue, D. W., Sue, D., Neville, H. A., and Smith, L. (2019). *Counseling the culturally diverse: Theory and practice* (8th ed.). New York, NY: Wiley.

Sun, R. C., and Shek, D. T. (2010). Life satisfaction, positive youth development, and problem behaviour among Chinese adolescents in Hong Kong. *Social Indicators Research, 95*(3), 455–474. DOI: 10.1007/s11205-009-9531-9

Swearer, S. M., Espelage, D. L., Vaillancourt, T., Hymel, S. (2010). What can be done about school bullying? Linking research to educational practice. *Educational Researcher, 39*(1), 38–47. DOI: 10.3102/0013189X09357622

Tartakovsky, M. (2013). *10 practical tips for raising an emotionally healthy boy.* Retrieved from https://psychcentral.com/blog/10-practical-tips-for-raising-an-emotionally-healthy-boy/

Telford, R. M., Telford, R. D., Olive, L. S., Cochrane, T., Davey, R. (2016). *Why are girls less physically active than boys? Findings from the LOOK longitudinal study.* DOI: 10.1371/journal.pone.0150041

Tembon, M., and Fort, L. (2008). *Girls' education in the 21st century: Gender equality, empowerment, and economic growth.* Retrieved from https://siteresources.worldbank.org/EDUCATION/Resources/278200-1099079877269/547664-1099080014368/DID_Girls_edu.pdf

Testa, R. J., Jiminez, C. L., and Rankin, S. (2014). Risk and resilience during transgender identity development: The effects of awareness and engagement with other transgender people on affect. *Journal of Gay & Lesbian Mental Health, 18*(1), 31–46. DOI: 10.1080/19359705.2013.805177

The Mentoring Center. (2018). *About us.* Retrieved from http://mentor.org/about-us/

Thoreson, R. R. (2016). "Like walking through a hailstorm": Discrimination against LGBT youth in US schools. *Human Rights Organization.* Retrieved from https://www.hrw.org/report/2016/12/07/walking-through-hailstorm/discrimination-against-lgbt-youth-us-schools

United Nations. (2017). *Population facts.* Retrieved from https://www.un.org/en/development/desa/population/publications/pdf/popfacts/PopFacts_2017-5.pdf

U.S. Census Bureau. (2017). *School enrollment in the United States: October 2016—detailed tables [Table 4].* Retrieved from https://www.census.gov/data/tables/2016/demo/school-enrollment/2016-cps.html

U.S. Department of the Interior (n.d.). *Tribal enrollment process.* Retrieved from https://www.doi.gov/tribes/enrollment

Vaillant, G. E. (1998). *Adaptation to life.* Cambridge, MA: Harvard University Press.

Vercelletto, C. (2016). Role reversal: Why our boys struggle in school. *Working Mother.* Retrieved from https://www.workingmother.com/content/role-reversal-why-our-boys-struggle-school

Vernon, A., and Schimmel, C. J. (2018). *Counseling children and adolescents* (fifth ed.). San Diego, CA: Cognella Academic Publishing.

Vitelli, R. (2017). *Do fathers treat their sons and daughters differently?* Retrieved from https://www.psychologytoday.com/us/blog/media-spotlight/201706/do-fathers-treat-their-sons-and-daughters-differently

Walsh, D. (2014). *Why do they act that way? A survival guide to the adolescent brain for you and your teen.* New York, NY: Atria Books.

Warble, F. (2018). *Oh boy! Strategies for teaching boys in early childhood.* Lincoln, NE: Exchange Press.

Warella, E., Rideout, V., Montague, H., Beaudion-Ryan, L., and Lauricella, A. R. (2016). Teens, health and technology: A national survey. *Media and Communication, 4*(3), 13–23. DOI: 10.17645/macv4i3.515

Waters, M. C., and Pineau, M. G. (2015). *The integration of immigrants into American society.* Washington, DC: The National Academies Press.

Weinberg, M. K., Tronick, E. Z., Cohn, J. F., and Olson, K. L. (1999). Gender differences in emotional expressivity and self-regulation during early infancy. *Developmental Psychology, 35*(1), 175–188. DOI: 10.1037/0012-1649.35.1.175

Weir, K. (2017). *Maximizing children's resilience.* Retrieved from https://www.apa.org/monitor/2017/09/cover-resilience

Wilson, T. D., Reinhard, D. A., Westgate, E. C., Gilbert, D. T., Ellerbeck, N., Hahn, C., and Shaked, A. (2014). Just think: The challenges of the disengaged mind. *Science, 345*(6192), 75–77. DOI: 10.1126/science.1250830

Winston, R., and Chicot, R. (2016). The importance of early bonding on the long-term mental health and resilience of children. *London Journal of Primary Care, 8*(1), 12–14. DOI: 10.1080/17571472.2015.1133012

Winters, M. F. (2015). Who am I? Part 4: Native American identity development. *The Inclusion Solution.* Retrieved from www.theinclusionsolution.me/who-am-i-part-4-native-american-identity-development/

Wong, A. (2018). *Boys don't read enough.* Retrieved from https://www.theatlantic.com/education/archive/2018/09/why-girls-are-better-reading-boys/571429/

Woolston, C. (2017). *Ten tips for raising a well-rounded boy.* Retrieved from https://www.babycenter.com/0_10-tips-for-raising-a-well-rounded-boy_10310246.bc

Worthington, R. L., Savoy, H., Dillon, F. R., and Vernalia, E. R. (2002). Heterosexual identity development: A multidimensional model of individual and group identity. *The Counseling Psychologist, 30*(4), 496–531. DOI: 10.1177/00100002030004002

Wright, B. L. (2011). I know who I am, do you? Identity and academic achievement of successful African American male adolescents in an urban pilot high school in the United States. *Urban Education, 46*(4), 611–638. DOI: 10.1177/0042085911400319

Wyss, S. E. (2004). "This was my hell": The violence experienced by gender non-conforming youth in US high schools. *International Journal of Qualitative Studies in Education, 17*(5), 709–730. Retrieved from http://www.postpresby.org/jkoch/Intro/Readings/Gender%20Hell.pdf

Yalom, I., and Leszcz, M. (2005). *The theory and practice of group psychotherapy* (fifth ed.). New York, NY: Basic Books.

Yavosky, J. E., Buchmann, C., and Miles, A. (2015). *High school boys, gender, and academic achievement: Does masculinity negatively impact boys' grade point averages?* Retrieved from https://paa2015.princeton.edu/papers/152814

Yogman, M., and Garfield, C. F. (2016). Fathers' roles in the care and development of their children: The role of pediatricians. *Pediatrics, 138*(1), 1128–1133. DOI: 10.1542/peds.2016-1128

Young, N. D., and Jean, E. (2018a). Penciling in parents: Making time for partnerships that count. In N. D. Young, E. Jean, and T. A. Citro. *From Head to Heart: High Quality Teaching Practices in the Spotlight* (pp.107–120). Wilmington, DE: Vernon Press.

Young, N. D., and Jean, E. (2018b). Supporting struggling students on campus: An academic recipe for success. In N. D. Young, A. Fain, and T. A. Citro, *Turbulent times: Confronting challenges in emerging adulthood* (pp. 135–146). Madison, WI: Atwood Publishing.

Young, N. D., Jean, E., and Mead, A. (2018). *Potency of the principalship*. Wilmington, DE: Vernon Press.

Youth Collaboratory. (2018). *Trauma-informed mentoring*. Retrieved from https://youthcollaboratory.org/resource/trauma-informed-mentoring

Zeff, T. (2013). *Raise an emotionally healthy boy: Save your son from the violent boy culture*. San Ramon, CA: Prana Publishing.

About the Authors

Dr. Nicholas D. Young has worked in diverse educational roles for more than thirty years, serving as a teacher, counselor, principal, special education director, graduate professor, graduate program director, graduate dean, and longtime psychologist and superintendent of schools. He was named the Massachusetts Superintendent of the Year, and he completed a distinguished Fulbright program focused on the Japanese educational system through the collegiate level. Dr. Young is the recipient of numerous other honors and recognitions including the General Douglas MacArthur Award for distinguished civilian and military leadership and the Vice Admiral John T. Hayward Award for exemplary scholarship. He holds several graduate degrees including a PhD in educational administration and an EdD in educational psychology.

Dr. Young has served in the U.S. Army and U.S. Army Reserves combined for over thirty-four years. He graduated with distinction from the U.S. Air War College, the U.S. Army War College, and the U.S. Navy War College. After completing a series of senior leadership assignments in the U.S. Army Reserves as the commanding officer of the 287th Medical Company (DS), the 405th Area Support Company (DS), the 405th Combat Support Hospital, and the 399th Combat Support Hospital, he transitioned to his current military position as a faculty instructor at the U.S. Army War College in Carlisle, Pennsylvania. He currently holds the rank of colonel.

Dr. Young is also a regular presenter at state, national, and international conferences. He has written many books, book chapters, and/or articles on various topics in education, counseling, and psychology. Some of his most recent books include *Masculinity in the Making: Managing the Transition to Manhood* (in press); *The Special Education Toolbox: Supporting Exceptional Teachers, Students, and Families* (2019); *Sounding the Alarm in the School-*

house: Safety, Security and Student Well-Being (2019); *Creating Compassionate Classrooms: Understanding the Continuum of Disabilities and Effective Educational Interventions* (2019); *Acceptance, Understanding, and the Moral Imperative of Promoting Social Justice Education in the Schoolhouse* (2019); *Empathic Teaching: Promoting Social Justice in the Contemporary Classroom* (2019); *Educating the Experienced: Challenges and Best Practices in Adult Learning* (2019); *Securing the Schoolyard: Protocols that Promote Safety and Positive Student Behaviors* (2019); *The Soul of the Schoolhouse: Cultivating Student Engagement* (2018); *Embracing and Educating the Autistic Child: Valuing Those Who Color Outside the Lines* (2018); *From Cradle to Classroom: A Guide to Special Education for Young Children* (2018); *Captivating Classrooms: Educational Strategies to Enhance Student Engagement* (2018); *Potency of the Principalship: Action-Oriented Leadership at the Heart of School Improvement* (2018); *Soothing the Soul: Pursuing a Life of Abundance Through a Practice of Gratitude* (2018); *Dog Tags to Diploma: Understanding and Addressing the Educational Needs of Veterans, Servicemembers, and their Families* (2018); *Turbulent Times: Confronting Challenges in Emerging Adulthood* (2018); *Guardians of the Next Generation: Igniting the Passion for Quality Teaching* (2018); *Achieving Results: Maximizing Success in the Schoolhouse* (2018); *From Head to Heart: High Quality Teaching Practices in the Spotlight* (2018); *Stars in the Schoolhouse: Teaching Practices and Approaches that Make a Difference* (2018); *Making the Grade: Promoting Positive Outcomes for Students with Learning Disabilities* (2018); *Paving the Pathway for Educational Success: Effective Classroom Interventions for Students with Learning Disabilities* (2018); *Wrestling with Writing: Effective Strategies for Struggling Students* (2018); *Floundering to Fluent: Reaching and Teaching the Struggling Student* (2018); *Emotions and Education: Promoting Positive Mental Health in Students with Learning Disabilities* (2018); *From Lecture Hall to Laptop: Opportunities, Challenges, and the Continuing Evolution of Virtual Learning in Higher Education* (2017); *The Power of the Professoriate: Demands, Challenges, and Opportunities in 21st Century Higher Education* (2017); *To Campus with Confidence: Supporting a Successful Transition to College for Students with Learning Disabilities* (2017); *Educational Entrepreneurship: Promoting Public-Private Partnerships for the 21st Century* (2015); *Beyond the Bedtime Story: Promoting Reading Development during the Middle School Years* (2015); *Betwixt and Between: Understanding and Meeting the Social and Emotional Developmental Needs of Students During the Middle School Transition Years* (2014); *Learning Style Perspectives: Impact Upon the Classroom* (3rd ed., 2014); *Collapsing Educational Boundaries from Preschool to PhD: Building Bridges Across the Educational Spectrum* (2013); *Transforming Special Education Practices: A Primer for School Administrators and Policy Makers* (2012); and *Powerful Partners in*

Student Success: Schools, Families and Communities (2012). He also coauthored several children's books to include the popular series I am Full of Possibilities. Dr. Young may be contacted directly at nyoung1191@aol.com.

Dr. Christine N. Michael is a more than forty-year educational veteran with a variety of professional experiences. She holds degrees from Brown University, Rhode Island College, Union Institute and University, and the University of Connecticut, where she earned a PhD in education, human development, and family relations. Her previous work has included middle and high school teaching, higher education administration, college teaching, and educational consulting. She has also been involved with Head Start, Upward Bound, national nonprofits Foundation for Excellent Schools and College for Every Student, and the federal Trio programs. She is currently program director of Low Residency Programs at American International College.

Dr. Michael has published widely on topics in education and psychology. Her most recent works included serving as a primary author on the book *Masculinity in the Making: Managing the Transition to Manhood* (in press); *Securing the Schoolyard: Protocols that Promote Safety and Positive Student Behaviors* (2019); *Sounding the Alarm in the Schoolhouse: Safety, Security and Student Well-Being* (2019); *The Soul of the Schoolhouse: Cultivating Student Engagement* (2019); *Captivating Classrooms: Educational Strategies to Enhance Student Engagement* (2019); *Turbulent Times: Confronting Challenges in Emerging Adulthood* (2018); *To Campus with Confidence: Supporting a Successful Transition to College for Students with Learning Disabilities* (2017); *Beyond the Bedtime Story: Promoting Reading Development during the Middle School Years* (2015); *Betwixt and Between: Understanding and Meeting the Social and Emotional Development Needs of Students During the Middle School Transition Years* (2014); and *Powerful Partners in Student Success: Schools, Families and Communities* (2012). Dr. Michael may be contacted at cnevadam@gmail.com.

Dr. Elizabeth Jean has served as an elementary school educator and administrator in various rural and urban settings in Massachusetts for more than twenty years. As a building administrator, she has fostered partnerships with staff, families, various local businesses, and higher education institutions. Further, she is currently a graduate adjunct professor at the Van Loan School of Education, Endicott College, and previously taught at the College of Our Lady of the Elms. In terms of formal education, Dr. Jean received a BS in education from Springfield College; an MEd in education with a concentration in reading from the College of Our Lady of the Elms; and an EdD in curriculum, teaching, learning, and leadership from Northeastern University.

Dr. Jean is a primary author on *Masculinity in the Making: Managing the Transition to Manhood* (in press); *Acceptance, Understanding, and the Mo-*

ral Imperative of Promoting Social Justice Education in the School-house (2019); *The Empathic Teacher: Learning and Applying the Principles of Social Justice Education to the Classroom* (2019); *From Cradle to Classroom: A Guide to Special Education for Young Children* (2019); *The Potency of the Principalship: Action-Oriented Leadership at the Heart of School Improvement* (2018); *Dog Tags to Diploma: Understanding and Addressing the Educational Needs of Veterans, Servicemembers, and their Families* (2018); *Stars in the Schoolhouse: Teaching Practices and Approaches that Make a Difference* (2018); *From Head to Heart: High Quality Teaching Practices in the Spotlight* (2018); *From Lecture Hall to Laptop: Opportunities, Challenges, and the Continuing Evolution of Virtual Learning in Higher Education* (2017). She has also written book chapters on such topics as emotional well-being for students with learning disabilities, post-secondary campus supports for emerging adults, parental supports for students with learning disabilities, home-school partnerships, virtual education, public and private partnerships in public education, professorial pursuits, technology partnerships between P–12 and higher education, developing a strategic mindset for LD students, the importance of skill and will in developing reading habits for young children, and middle school reading interventions to name a few. Additionally, she has coauthored and illustrated several children's books to include *Yes, Mama* (2018), *The Adventures of Scotty the Skunk: What's that Smell?* (2014), and many of the I am Full of Possibilities series for Learning Disabilities Worldwide. She may be contacted at elizabethjean1221@gmail.com.